THE YELLOW TEXT

laügh

your way

through

grammar

Joan D. Berbrich, Ph.D.

Amsco books by Joan D. Berbrich

Fifteen Steps to Better Writing
Laugh Your Way Through Grammar:
    Blue, Yellow, Green
Macbeth: A Resource Book
101 Ways to Learn Vocabulary
Reading Around the World
Reading Today
Thirteen Steps to Better Writing
Wide World of Words
Writing About Amusing Things
Writing About Curious Things
Writing About Fascinating Things
Writing About People
Writing Creatively
Writing Logically
Writing Practically

THE YELLOW TEXT

laügh
your way
through
grammar

Dedicated to serving

our nation's youth

Amsco School Publications, Inc.
315 Hudson Street/New York, N.Y. 10013

When ordering this book, please specify:
either **R 530 YS** or
LAUGH YOUR WAY THROUGH GRAMMAR
YELLOW TEXT, SOFTBOUND

ISBN 0-87720-794-1

To the Student

The English language is amazing!

You can move one space and transform poor Suzy . . .

from a lighthouse keeper to a light housekeeper.

Or add one capital letter and turn a minor accident into a criminal assault . . .

Tom was arrested for hitting a pole on Broadway.
Tom was arrested for hitting a Pole on Broadway.

Or introduce one period and change a negative to a positive . . .

No woman can be successful.
No. Woman can be successful.

Or change the placement of a single punctuation mark and change victory to defeat (as happened with the Oracle of Delphi) . . .

"Thou shalt go; thou shalt return;
never by war shalt thou perish."

"Thou shalt go; thou shalt return never;
by war shalt thou perish."

Or simply shift the emphasis and change the meaning of an entire sentence . . .

Baby swallows fly. (natural history)
Baby swallows fly. (better call a doctor!)

The English language is fun. Because it is rich and varied, because it is still alive and changing, you can do all sorts of things with it.

You can reverse letters and create glorious nonsense . . .

You can grow a YAM in MAY,
take a ROOM on a MOOR,
or change a REED to a DEER.

Or reverse pairs of words and change occupations . . .

> someone who SAILS SHIPS and someone who SHIPS SAILS,
> someone who PAINTS SHELVES and someone who SHELVES
> PAINTS.

You can have a ball with visual phrases . . .

> When you PUNCH A CLOCK, does your fist hurt?
> When you join a CAR POOL, are you swimming with Fords?

You can play with multiple meanings. A SLIDE may be . . .

> a piece of playground equipment,
> a photographic transparency, or
> something you do as you near home plate.

*In fact, you can play with multiple meanings and cause confusion—for
some words have two meanings, each of which contradicts the other . . .*

> When you DUST, you *remove* something from furniture
> but *add* something to crops.

You can use homonyms in nonsensical wordplay . . .

> Off the coast of WALES, wearing corduroys with WALES,
> she spotted a school of WHALES, all chanting WAILS.

*You can develop simple anagrams (words formed by scrambling the letters
of other words) to turn . . .*

> GULP into PLUG—or MILE into LIME

. . . or complex anagrams to turn . . .

> THE DETECTIVES into people who DETECT THIEVES
> or
> GOLD AND SILVER into GRAND OLD EVILS.

This wordplay, this ability to have verbal fun, is possible only if you
become truly familiar with our common language. Of course, wordplay is
serious, too. You are playing with words every time you write a sentence.
You choose particular words, and you choose to order them in a particular
way. The result is your personal style (or—sadly—lack of style!).

This text is designed to make you more sensitive, more alert, more knowledgeable about serious wordplay (sometimes called grammar!) and—at the same time—to increase your skills with amusing wordplay: in other words, to help you have fun with words.

Many of the sentences used in the text proper (Sections II through V) and most of the sentences used in the Practice Sessions (Section I) are based on jokes, riddles, quips, or trivia items. They should appeal to your funny bone, hold your interest, and make grammar "user-friendly." (For those of you who are not hackers, the hyphenated expression is computer lingo!)

We hope this book will do what it is designed to do—to help you to a mastery of the English language as you chuckle—giggle—and LAUGH YOUR WAY THROUGH GRAMMAR!

Instructions for the Practice Sessions

There is no easy road to good grammar . . . but there are roads that are interesting, challenging, and even—fun! Here's how to travel the particular road provided in this text.

1. Turn to Practice Session (PS) 1. Notice the title: "Mixed Bag." This title tells you that you can expect to find *any* type of error in this PS: grammar, usage, punctuation, capitalization, even spelling. PS 2, on the other hand, bears the title: "Sentence Structure." This title tells you that the errors in this PS are limited to sentence structure errors.

2. Read the directions given directly under the title. Directions will vary from PS to PS, so it is important that you understand what you are expected to do.

3. Now you are ready for the first problem. Read sentence #1 of PS 1. Can you spot the error? Remember—since this PS is a "Mixed Bag," you will have to be alert for all types of errors. If you find the error quickly, good for you! If you don't (or if you want to check your answer), look at the reference number (in parentheses) which follows the sentence. In this case the number is 10-b.

4. Next turn to the text proper (Sections II–V). Look for #10 (page 66). When you find it, you will discover that #10 covers the four types of sentences. Check part "b." It tells you what an interrogative sentence is and how to punctuate one. Now—looking back at the first sentence in PS 1, you will see that "Did you hear that the flea circus went bankrupt because the leading lady ran off with a poodle" is, of course, an interrogative sentence and must be followed by a question mark. All clear?

5. Follow this same procedure with the rest of the sentences in PS 1. If you own this book, you may place a check mark to the left of any sentence you were unable to correct. **If you do not own this book, do not write in it.** Instead, enter the error in your notebook. You should quickly learn your strong and weak points: the rules you know and the rules you don't know. And this, in turn, will help you to concentrate on your own grammatical idiosyncrasies.

Summary: Please notice that you are *not* being asked to learn great blocks of grammar. You are *not* being asked to memorize 500 rules. You are *not* being asked to wade through exercises of ten, or twenty, or thirty sentences with the same type of error until you nod with boredom. Instead, you are being asked to be your own physician: to diagnose, to understand, and to correct. While you enjoy the content of the sentences in the Practice Sessions, you will discover your own grammatical weaknesses and will learn how to overcome them.

We hope you will do each Practice Session not once but many times. First work with each PS thoroughly. Then, as you browse a second, a third, or a tenth time through familiar jokes and fascinating facts, continue the procedure, detecting errors, correcting them, checking them in the text proper. You will learn easily and painlessly (at least we hope you will), and the result should be better speech, better writing, and a more sophisticated sense of humor.

ENJOY . . . .

If your teacher insists that spelling correctly is a snap, pass on this bit of doggerel. (The author's pen name is Anonymous.)

SPELLING FOOFARAW*

Let's consider the F—it's a devious sound:
Sometimes standing alone, as in iF or in Found;

Sometimes turning to twins, as in cliFF or in stiFF,
Or trailing the E in your best handkerchiEF;

Sometimes looking a bit like a P & H clone
As in PHillip and PHobia, PHoenix and PHone;

Sometimes lurking within an odd G & H blend
With lauGHter and couGH, as a rare dividend.

Sometimes skulking behind an L & F mask
As in caLF and in haLF. Now what did you ask?

Small wonder our students find spelling a chore,
When they are (Foiled, GHoiled, PHoiled, FFoiled?) by
       the F—evermore!

*a disturbance or fuss over a trifle

Joan D. Berbrich

ix

Contents

For a more detailed Table of Contents in any section,
turn to the first page of that section.

SECTION I
Practice Sessions

Continued on Following Page

PRACTICE SESSION 1—Mixed Bag

Each sentence below contains an error. Find it; understand why it is wrong; know how to correct it.

1. Did you hear that the flea circus went bankrupt because the leading lady ran off with a poodle. **(10-b)**

2. Tourists regularly kiss the Blarney Stone. In Cork, Ireland. **(12-d)**

3. Do not use run-on sentences they are hard to read! **(13-c)**

4. A skillet is a frying pan that has become some snobbish! **(189)**

5. Wrinkles are hereditary, parents get them from their children. **(14-c)**

6. Sign in restaurant: "Wanted: a man to wash dishes and two waitresses." **(15-a)**

7. Why didn't Noah swat both flys while he had the chance? **(23-b)**

8. It's very easy to see through people who insist on making spectacles of theirselves! **(27)**

9. Some of them snails have over 27,000 teeth. **(37-d)**

10. Jake and her told us that "Old Blue Eyes" is the nickname of Frank Sinatra. **(33-b, e.1)**

11. The trouble with blind love is that it don't stay that way! **(127)**

12. Watermelon is filled with water because its planted in the spring! **(35-c)**

13. My sister she buys her clothes on the installment plan so she's always dressed on time! **(37-b)**

14. When winter digged in, Harry used a snow shovel to dig out. **(41-b)**

15. I received a "D" in English, and that ain't fair! **(84)**

16. Antique dealers get mad when they're asked: "What's new?" **(95)**

17. If a mechanic turns musician the result is usually "car-tunes." **(224-g)**

18. Jenny thought that her family's last name was Hilton—because that was the name on they're towels. **(194)**

PRACTICE SESSION 2—Sentence Structure

Each sentence below contains a sentence structure error. (Review #10, 11, 12, 13, 14.) Identify each error; understand it; correct it.

1. In February, 1878, the New Haven District Telephone Company published the first telephone book it contained only fifty names. **(13-b)**

2. A coward is like a leaky faucet, they both run! **(14-d)**

3. Jed has a mind like blotting paper. Soaks up everything he hears but gets it backwards. **(12-a)**

4. You are never fully dressed. Until you wear a smile. **(12-d)**

5. Cross a homing pigeon and a parrot, if the pigeon gets lost, it can ask its way home. **(14-c)**

6. The oldest comic strip still in existence is "The Katzenjammer Kids" it first appeared in newspapers in 1897. **(13-d)**

7. Although the man who invented football got a kick out of it! **(12-c)**

8. Don't watch the clock, do what it does. Keep going! **(14-d)**

9. The oldest city in the world is probably Jericho about 3,000 people lived there in 7800 B.C. **(13-c)**

10. A lawyer is someone who can dictate ninety pages of material. And call it a brief! **(12-f)**

11. Charles Schulz must be a great botanist, for years he has worked on Peanuts! **(14-a)**

12. The Air Force turned me down I get dizzy when I wear high heels! **(13-d)**

13. Autumn being that time of the year when the days are getting shorter and the shorts are getting longer. **(12-b)**

14. The modern house is full of plants the modern garden is full of furniture! **(13-d)**

15. The poor have sore throats, the rich have acute laryngitis. **(14-d)**

16. In 1903 the first automobile to cross the U.S. took fifty-two days. To go from San Francisco to New York. **(12-d)**

17. Since John Lennon adopted the nickname "Ono" in 1969. **(12-c)**

PRACTICE SESSION 3—Mixed Bag

Each sentence below contains an error. Find it; understand it; correct it.

1. I'm taking trombone lessons, someone told me it's the only instrument on which you can get anywhere by letting things slide.   **(14-a)**

2. Our friends grumbled to theirselves that Barbie couldn't cook, but she could certainly dish it out!   **(27)**

3. Maine is the world's most largest producer of toothpicks.   **(56-c)**

4. My cousin, who I escorted to church, said the thing she likes about the church is the ''hims''!   **(30-d.2)**

5. Too many young people grow wishbones. Where their backbones should be.   **(12-e)**

6. Silly Suzy took the cake from the plate and ate it.   **(36-h)**

7. Some of them parents tie up their dogs and let their kids run loose!   **(37-d)**

8. He claims he just got a bright idea. Larry and me told him it was beginner's luck!   **(33-b, e.1)**

9. Just after the bell rung, my friend said that school is sChOOL!   **(41-b)**

10. I've never belonged to no club, so I've never had a club sandwich.   **(63-c)**

11. Remember to never split an infinitive.   **(48-a)**

12. Archie has hang-ups about everything accept his clothes!   **(77)**

13. ''Oh, this new chocolate pizza tastes marvelously!'' said Mabel.   **(63-e)**

14. I must of spilled some of this new hair tonic on my comb—now it's a brush!   **(119)**

15. In Virginia, it was once illegal to have a bathtub inside of a house; it had to be kept in the yard.   **(152)**

16. When school principles retire, they lose their faculties!   **(180)**

17. The cranium is one room that never gets real crowded.   **(184)**

18. An octopus not only has eight legs but also blue blood.   **(20-k)**

PRACTICE SESSION 4—Spelling

Which word in each set of parentheses is spelled correctly?

1. "You used," Tim said pompously, "an (unecessary, unnecessary) comma!" **(232-a)**

2. Crime wouldn't pay if we let the (goverment, government) run it. **(233-a)**

3. "$ucce$$" always ends with twice as many dollars as it has at the (begining, beginning). **(233-d)**

4. The check you sent I (received, recieved) twice: once from you and once from the bank. **(234-c)**

5. When we were (picnicing, picnicking) in North Africa, some natives told us that there they call a rainbow "the bride of the rain." **(236)**

6. (Bookeepers, Bookkeepers) have great figures! **(237)**

7. It isn't surprising that the (calendar, calender) is sad—its days are numbered! **(237)**

8. The only way to be the winner in an (argument, arguement) is to avoid it. **(237)**

9. Sentiment has no place in (business, bussiness)—except for the person who sells greeting cards. **(237)**

10. When the patient complained that he was always (forgeting, forgetting) things, the psychiatrist quickly suggested he pay in advance! **(233-d)**

11. The most difficult (freight, frieght) train to catch is the 12:50 because it's ten to one if you catch it! **(234-d)**

12. If you can't resist snacking, just remember that (monkeys, monkies) like to eat every ninety minutes! **(23-c)**

13. My favorite book is *The (Arctic, Artic) Ocean* by I. C. Waters! **(237)**

14. "Doing (arithmatic, arithmetic) problems is tiring," said Gullible Gus, "because of all the numbers you have to carry!" **(237)**

15. You can get into a locked (cematery, cemetery) by using a skeleton key! **(238)**

16. If a dentist (does'nt, doesn't) take pains, the patient will. **(237)**

PRACTICE SESSION 5—Noun Plurals and Apostrophes

(Review #23.) Preceding each sentence is a singular noun. What is its plural form?

1. **(stitch)** "Surgeons are like comedians," said Gullible Gus. "They keep people in __?__." **(23-a)**

2. **(chimney)** The big chimney told the little __?__ they were too small to—smoke! **(23-c)**

3. **(passerby)** Half a dozen __?__ chuckled when the street comic said that Henry VIII liked to watch baseball games—especially double-headers! **(23-l)**

4. **(goose)** The poet Lord Byron had four pet __?__ that he took with him wherever he went. **(23-h)**

5. **(child)** Some __?__ consider spanking as "stern" punishment! **(23-g)**

6. **(genius)** "There have been only two __?__ in the world: Willie Mays and Willie Shakespeare." (Tallulah Bankhead) **(23-a)**

7. **(leaf)** If money grew on trees, raking __?__ would be fun. **(23-f)**

8. **(potato)** She's a portrait painter—always trying to turn __?__ into peaches! **(23-e)**

9. **(spoonful)** Recipe for an astronaut: take a cupful of courage, add three __?__ of recklessness, and spice with stars. **(23-m)**

(Review #24.) In each sentence find the error and know how to correct it.

10. Silly Suzy thinks that Joan of Arc was Noahs wife! **(24-a)**

11. If you want to forget others faults, remember your own! **(24-d)**

12. The only thing he ever did for a living was read his father-in-laws will! **(24-e)**

13. Bert has never done a days work—he's a night watchman. **(24-a)**

14. In 1964, Baskin-Robbins created Beatle Nut ice cream to celebrate the Beatles arrival here for their first American tour. **(24-d)**

PRACTICE SESSION 6—Mixed Bag

In each sentence find the error; understand it; correct it.

1. If you want to kill time, why not try working it to death.   **(10-b)**

2. Do you know whom first described a butterfly as "a caterpillar that has won its wings"?   **(30-d.1)**

3. Many Lapplanders have ranches where they raise reindeers for meat and milk.   **(23-i)**

4. Gullible Gus was so cold that he put on his blazer he figured the fire would keep him warm!   **(13-c)**

5. A is a letter that's always written in hAste!   **(225-b)**

6. Silly Suzy is so concieted that she claims the "F" on her report card stands for "Fantastic"!   **(234-c)**

7. Our parents told Ted and I that today's teenagers want life, liberty, and a car in which to pursue happiness!   **(34-b, d.2)**

8. Us campers know from sad experience that flies bite more just before it rains.   **(37-c)**

9. Twisted proverb: People who live in glass houses shouldnt take a bath!   **(226-a)**

10. Billboard: See where the Pilgrims landed by bus!   **(15-a)**

11. Petunia was aggravated when her boss offered her praise instead of a raise.   **(82)**

12. A fellow going nowheres can be sure of reaching his destination.   **(63-a)**

13. According to some Texans, TEXAS should always be spoken and written in capitol letters!   **(113)**

14. Mathematics are sometimes a problem for Yogi Berra. He once said: "Baseball is ninety percent mental. The other half is physical."   **(23-j)**

15. Fools rush in—and get the more better seats.   **(56-c)**

16. Next summer my brother and I are going on a fishing trip to King Salmon, Alaska Salmon, Idaho and Whitefish, Montana.   **(222-c)**

PRACTICE SESSION 7—Mixed Bag

Each sentence below contains an underlined expression. Below each sentence are four possible answers. Which one is correct?

1. Stained glass windows first appeared in <u>churches, they</u> next appeared in Mississippi steamboats.   **(23-a, 14-a)**

   a. Correct as is
   b. churchs; they

   c. churches.They
   d. churches they

2. The two walls said to <u>one another: "I'll</u> meet you at the corner." **(128, 223-c)**

   a. Correct as is
   b. each other: "I'll

   c. one another. "I'll
   d. each other. "I'll

3. "By the mid-1900's, the Library of Congress contained over 200 miles of <u>bookshelfs,"</u> Jennifer said gravely.   **(23-f, 225-g)**

   a. Correct as is
   b. bookshelfs",

   c. bookshelves,"
   d. bookshelves",

4. In <u>Ken and Liz's</u> new play, nothing happens for the first fifteen minutes. It's for people who come to the theater late!   **(24-f)**

   a. Correct as is
   b. Ken's and Liz's

   c. Kens' and Lizs'
   d. Ken's and Liz

5. "Human blood—which contains iron—is red," Dr. Smith told <u>Nora and I, and</u> octopus blood—which contains copper—is blue." **(34-a, d.1, 225-a)**

   a. Correct as is
   b. Nora and me, and

   c. Nora and I, "and
   d. Nora and me, "and

6. This is the computer age, and one of my <u>buddies have</u> a chip on his shoulder!   **(23-b, 47-h)**

   a. Correct as is
   b. buddys has

   c. buddies has
   d. buddys have

7. When the landlord said that he was going to raise her <u>rent my freind</u> was glad—because SHE couldn't raise it!   **(11-c, 234-b)**

   a. Correct as is
   b. rent, my freind

   c. rent; my friend
   d. rent, my friend

PRACTICE SESSION 8—Case of Personal Pronouns

Which pronoun in each set of parentheses is correct? Why? (Review #26-27, 32-35.)

1. That actor is in the middle of a great love affair—with (himself, hisself)! **(27)**

2. (Her, She) and Silly Suzy rose early to do their homework so that if they didn't know an answer, it would soon dawn on them! **(33-b, e.1)**

3. May my fellow debaters and (I, me) point out that a political war is one in which everyone shoots from the lip? **(33-b, c, e.1)**

4. This jingle is a favorite of (ours, our's): "Early to bed and early to rise won't help you much if you don't advertise!" **(35-b)**

5. Could it have been (her, she) who said that nothing lasts longer than a box of cereal that you don't like? **(33-c, d)**

6. A baseball team is like a pancake: (its, it's) success depends on the batter! **(35-c)**

7. My father told Jimmy and (I, me) that profanity is an escape route for someone who has run out of ideas. **(34-b, d.2)**

8. Are you sure it was (her, she) who told you that for Kermit the Frog a good epitaph would be—"Croaked"? **(33-d)**

9. It took so long for my sisters and (I, me) to get out of the baseball parking lot that the people on the way in were football fans! **(34c, d.3)**

10. Why can't Lily and (I, me) write our report about William Butler Yeats and George Bernard Shaw, both poor spellers? **(33-b, c, e.1)**

11. It was (her, she) who said that gossip is brewing at every coffee break! **(33-d)**

12. According to (he, him) and his brother, some people like to ride in elevators because it raises their spirits! **(34-c, d.3)**

13. That house of (theirs, their's) is all-electric: everything in it is charged! **(35-b)**

14. If you can believe (her, she) and her brother, every teenager has a secret desire to write—checks! **(34-a)**

PRACTICE SESSION 9—Colon and Semicolon

In each sentence find the error; understand it; correct it. (Review #222, 223.)

1. Silly Suzy doesn't file her fingernails, she just throws them away! **(222-a)**

2. Many towns in the U.S. have "colorful names": Blue Springs, Missouri, Whitehall, Ohio, Golden, Colorado, and Red Wing, Minnesota. **(222-c)**

3. About talking, learn from the whale, it gets harpooned only when it comes up to spout! **(223-b)**

4. "Rhode Island and Providence Plantations" is the official name of Rhode Island hence the smallest state has the largest name! **(13, 222-b)**

5. Ann Landers, everybody's advisor, once wrote "Television has proved that people will look at anything rather than at each other." **(223-c)**

6. At 11.59 p.m., Leon made his final quip of the old year when he suggested that Sigmund Freud was symbol-minded! **(223-e)**

7. Only three words in the English language end in "-ceed," exceed, proceed, and succeed. **(223-a)**

8. Masquerade parties are prohibited by law in New York City however, they're illegal only in public places. **(13, 222-b)**

9. Alexander Graham Bell never had a teenager, as a result, he invented the telephone! **(14, 222-b)**

10. Small boy: "If I'm noisy, Mom gives me a spanking and if I'm quiet, she takes my temperature!" **(11-b.1, 222-c)**

11. Rich foods are our destiny, they shape our "ends"! **(14, 223-b)**

12. My cousin Alicia bought a waterbed, lately she seems to be drifting away. **(14, 222-a)**

13. Rabbi Dr. R. Brasch once said; "To know what a man is really like, observe what he is doing when he has nothing to do." **(223-c)**

14. "Goodbye" is a portmanteau word a blending of "God" and "be" (with) and "ye." **(223-b)**

PRACTICE SESSION 10—Punctuation Makes a Difference!

Is punctuation important? See for yourself! Can you explain clearly the difference between the two sentences in each of the following pairs?

1. Let's eat, Wilhelmina, and then go to the Mall.
   Let's eat Wilhelmina, and then go to the Mall.

2. The athlete, violently rejected by his fans and his children, moved to the North Pole.
   The athlete, violently rejected by his fans, and his children moved to the North Pole.

3. Helena, Montana, is 4,155 feet above sea level and is sometimes called "The Queen of the Mountains."
   Helena, Montana is 4,155 feet above sea level and is sometimes called "The Queen of the Mountains."

4. For Sale: Airplane, ticket, and carry-on bag, $55.
   For Sale: Airplane ticket and carry-on bag, $55.

5. "The grizzly bear," said the trainer, "is cantankerous."
   The grizzly bear said the trainer is cantankerous.

6. Tell your wife you're the boss.
   Tell your wife, "You're the boss."

7. Today only: 50% off on shoes, ladies' clothing, and wallets.
   Today only: 50% off on shoes, ladies, clothing, and wallets.

8. The play ended, happily.
   The play ended happily.

9. Melissa bought a book for $10.00.
   Melissa bought a book for $1,000.

10. As the burglar prowled, inside the children crouched in terror.
    As the burglar prowled inside, the children crouched in terror.

11. The lawyer purchased a little-used plane.
    The lawyer purchased a little used plane.

12. We hate fools; like you, we find them boring.
    We hate fools like you; we find them boring.

13. "Mr. Wallace," said Mr. Green, "is our new manager."
    Mr. Wallace said Mr. Green is our new manager.

PRACTICE SESSION 11—Mixed Bag

Each sentence below contains an underlined expression. Below each sentence are four possible answers. Which one is correct?

1. I send appropriate pets to celebritys; flying fish to the Wright brothers and a polo pony to Marco Polo.   (23-b, 223-b)

   a. Correct as is   c. celebritys:
   b. celebrities;   d. celebrities:

2. Gullible Gus said that his girlfriend's a twin, but he can identify her easy. Because her brother has a beard!   (63-d, 12-e)

   a. Correct as is   c. easily because
   b. easy because   d. easily. Because

3. Marriage, according to one authority whom I know, is the mathematics by which 1 + 1 equals 2, 3, 4, or more!   (30-d.2, 224-p)

   a. Correct as is   c. who I know, is
   b. whom I know is   d. who I know is

4. When he was a student at the Royal College Louis Pasteur was rated as "mediocre" in chemistry.   (11-c, 237)

   a. Correct as is   c. College, Louis
   b. Colledge, Louis   d. college Louis

5. The sun is like a good loaf of bread—its light when it rises!   (35-c, 227-d)

   a. Correct as is   c. bread, its
   b. bread—it's   d. bread, it's

6. What has she all ready grown if she has worked hard in her garden? (Answer: tired)   (90, 41-b)

   a. Correct as is   c. already grown
   b. all ready growed   d. already growed

7. Lope de Vega, the Spanish playwright, wrote 2,200 plays, but less then 500 survive.   (136, 195)

   a. Correct as is   c. fewer then
   b. fewer than   d. less than

PRACTICE SESSION 12—Capitalization

Which word in each set of parentheses is correct? (Review #206–219.)

1. Dizzy Dot thinks that the St. Louis (cardinals, Cardinals) are appointed by the Pope!   **(212-a)**

2. "Just call me Jack," said one crossing guard, "(since, Since) I'm forever holding up cars!"   **(209-b)**

3. About 5,000 of the 35,000 cowboys herding cattle along the old Chisholm (trail, Trail) were black.   **(211-a)**

4. Silly Suzy speaks with a (southern, Southern) accent because she drinks from Dixie cups!   **(211-c)**

5. The first ten amendments to the U.S. (constitution, Constitution) is called the Bill of Rights.   **(210-c)**

6. The clerk at the ski resort asked the guest for name, address, and Blue Cross (number, Number).   **(212-c)**

7. The popular retort, "Be my guest," was originally the slogan of Conrad Hilton, the (hotel, Hotel) tycoon.   **(22-b)**

8. If you think (high school, High School) is boring, wait until you sit around an unemployment office!   **(213-a)**

9. Classroom boner: In (biology, Biology) class, I learned that a lack of vitamins causes "crickets"!   **(213-b)**

10. When I was a (senior, Senior) in high school, I learned that Theodore Roosevelt, our twenty-sixth President, had written forty books. **(213-c)**

11. Other books inform us; the (bible, Bible) transforms us.   **(214-c)**

12. My (brother, Brother) John says that washing behind the ears is an all-day project—for an elephant!   **(215-a)**

13. The metric system was legalized in 1866 by (president, President) Andrew Johnson.   **(215-b)**

14. My head is like a computer, (dad, Dad)—but I think there's been a power shortage!   **(215-c)**

15. Alice Roosevelt Longworth said this about Calvin Coolidge: "(he, He) looks as if he had been weaned on a pickle."   **(209-a)**

PRACTICE SESSION 13—Mixed Bag

In each sentence find the error; understand it; correct it.

1. The sidewalks in winter being like music—because if you don't C-sharp, you will B-flat! **(12-b)**

2. According to she and her brother, in Europe they saw a house mouse that sings like a canary. **(34-c, d.3)**

3. The brand name "Noxzema" comes from it's claim: it knocks eczema. **(35-c)**

4. My friend she said she didn't want to read the dictionary—she would wait until it was made into a movie! **(37-b)**

5. The alumnuses giggled when the speaker, a grammarian, said thoughtfully that a kiss is a noun that is both common and proper. **(23-o)**

6. The matador was some upset when he heard that bulls are not excited by the color red—in fact, they're colorblind! **(189)**

7. The giant squid has the largest eyes in the world—over fifteen inches across, bigger then a dinner plate. **(195)**

8. Once I had an English teacher who use to say that a literary critic is someone who finds meanings in a book that the author didn't know were there. **(200)**

9. R. P. Blackmur, a critic, once wrote that myths are merely "Gossip grown old." **(209-c)**

10. All right, governor, I admit that an apple pie without some cheese is like a kiss without a squeeze! **(215-c)**

11. The prizefighter Jack Johnson strolled along the streets of Paris with his pet leopard, the poet Baudelaire walked his favorite lobster on a leash. **(14-c)**

12. Why did Robert Heinlein call an elephant "a mouse built to government specifications?" **(225-g)**

13. Silly Suzy said that she wouldnt go to the moon if it were the last place on earth! **(226-a)**

14. Don't never try to throw away an old boomerang! **(63-c)**

15. If George Washington was so honest, how come all of the banks close on his birthday? **(85)**

PRACTICE SESSION 14—Confused Words

Which word in parentheses is correct?

1. A rich (desert, dessert) is something that spends a moment between your lips and a lifetime on your hips. **(121)**

2. Charles Creighton and James Hargis have probably driven in reverse (farther, further) than anyone else: they crossed the country, driving in reverse, in eighteen days! **(135)**

3. London's Scotland Yard pays a secretary to handle the mail addressed to the (famous, notorious) fictional character, Sherlock Holmes. **(172)**

4. College soon (learned, taught) me that not all educated people are intelligent! **(161)**

5. A hypocrite is someone who (prays, preys) on his knees on Sundays and (prays, preys) on his neighbors the rest of the week. **(179)**

6. (Irregardless, Regardless) of what you have heard, the pre-Inca Indians of Peru did worship peanut butter. **(153)**

7. Husband: When we were first married, I thought you were an (angel, angle). **(94)**
   Wife: Is that why you never bought me any new clothes?

8. Even (among, between) the ancient Egyptians, "Red" was a popular nickname. **(92)**

9. If you can't hear a pin drop, there's something wrong with (your, you're) bowling! **(205)**

10. An archeologist may be defined as "a person (who's, whose) career lies in ruins." **(204)**

11. Silly Suzy went outdoors with her purse open because she was expecting some change in the (weather, whether)! **(202)**

12. Max said that he (saw, seen) in a book that Einstein was four years old before he could speak and seven before he could read. **(186)**

13. North America was (formally, formerly) called "Turtle Island" by the Delaware Indians. **(138)**

14. A specialist is a doctor (who's, whose) patients are trained to become ill only during office hours. **(204)**

PRACTICE SESSION 15—Agreement of Pronoun and Antecedent

Which pronoun in parentheses is correct? Why? (Review #36.)

1. In the 1950's, one movie studio let the contracts of Clint Eastwood and Burt Reynolds expire because (it, they) felt that neither one showed much promise. **(26, 36-a)**

2. If someone's really clever, (she or he knows, they know) that the gift of gab is knowing when to listen. **(29-a, 36-c)**

3. The owner and the manager declared that (his, their) promise cannot be made more binding by using a lot of red tape. **(36-f.1)**

4. Everyone at the restaurant last night said that (he or she, they) loved what had been made for dinner—reservations! **(29-a, 36-c)**

5. My family—in (its, their) infinite wisdom—agreed unanimously that hash is the art of making ends "meat." **(36-e)**

6. The author and illustrator of the new novel said that (she considers, they consider) a book a success when people who haven't read it pretend they have! **(36-f.2)**

7. After the tea party, either Pat's parents or his uncle said that (he, they) had seen better conversations in alphabet soup! **(36-g.4)**

8. Each girl in our tour travels like Mrs. Noah—(she's, they've) taken along two of everything! **(36-d)**

Sometimes the antecedent of a pronoun is not clear. How would you revise each of the following sentences to eliminate the ambiguity? (See #36-h.)

9. When the president of the company was checking the treasurer's report, he really learned the nature of fear.

10. When Althea and Lauren were talking about their hobbies, she said that the soul is dyed the color of one's leisure hours.

11. As soon as the children cleared their plates, their mother put them into the dishwasher!

12. When Agatha and Kristin were watching television, she said that she thought the English Channel was the one on which you view British movies!

PRACTICE SESSION 16—Mixed Bag

Each sentence below contains an underlined expression. Below each sentence are four possible answers. Which one is correct?

1. It is the opinion of <u>he and his Cousin Ed</u> that a hitchhiker is one person who can be incapacitated by the loss of a thumb! **(34-c, d.3, 215-a)**

   a. Correct as is   *c.* him and his cousin Ed
   b. he and his cousin Ed   *d.* him and his Cousin Ed

2. Of all the <u>hobbys making</u> balls of rubberbands must surely give more bounce to the ounce! **(23-b, 224-h)**

   a. Correct as is   *c.* hobbies making
   b. hobbys making   *d.* hobbies, making

3. As I <u>past the laboratory,</u> I wondered if science would ever find a cure for the "foot-in-mouth" disease. **(176, 238)**

   a. Correct as is   *c.* past the labratory,
   b. passed the laboratory,   *d.* passed the labratory,

4. <u>Somewheres in high school</u> is a wit who insists that Eskimos keep their money in snowbanks! **(63-a, 213-a)**

   a. Correct as is   *c.* Somewheres in High School
   b. Somewhere in high school   *d.* Somewhere in High School

5. When the speaker said that nothing is impossible, one bright student chirped: "Have you ever tried to push toothpaste back <u>into the tube?"</u> **(151, 225-g)**

   a. Correct as is   *c.* in the tube?"
   b. into the tube"?   *d.* in the tube"?

6. Ed is the <u>kind of a person who</u> quips that mummies are Egyptians that were pressed for time! **(156, 203)**

   a. Correct as is   *c.* kind of person who
   b. kind of a person that   *d.* kind of person which

7. Golf is a good game for people eager to keep their health and <u>loose there temper!</u> **(166, 194)**

   a. Correct as is   *c.* loose their
   b. lose their   *d.* lose they're

PRACTICE SESSION 17—Verbs

Complete the following sentences by providing the past tense form of each verb in parentheses.   **(41-b, c, d)**

1. **(sing)** The air was so polluted yesterday that when Sally __?__ "I'm walking on air," she meant it!

2. **(spring)** I __?__ to my feet to remind the audience that Lyndon B. Johnson, when he was young, was so poor that he bought his future wife an engagement ring that cost less than $3.

3. **(strive)** I __?__ mightily not to laugh when little Jimmy said that a filly is a city in Pennsylvania.

4. **(drink)** The poor man always __?__ coffee because he had no proper tea (property)!

5. **(think)** Silly Suzy __?__ a coquette is a small Coke.

6. **(spread)** Yesterday I __?__ the news all over town that the doctor had X-rayed my brother's head and found—nothing!

Complete the following sentences by providing the past participle form of the verb in parentheses.

7. **(break)** Diets and promises have one thing in common—they're always being __?__!

8. **(burst)** Silly Suzy said that a laugh is a smile that has __?__ .

9. **(steal)** Newsflash: 500 wigs have been __?__ from a store in Detroit. Police are combing the area.

10. **(buy)** After his mother had __?__ him and his brother a double-decker bed, he said it was a lot of bunk!

11. **(write)** By 1987, Kathleen Lindsay had __?__ 904 novels under six pen names.

12. **(give)** Charles Dickens had a cat named William; after the cat had __?__ birth to a litter of kittens, William was renamed Williamina.

13. **(hurt)** It must have __?__ Caruso when his music teacher told him: "You can't sing. You have no voice at all."

14. **(read)** I have often __?__ that Hindus eat only with the right hand and drink only with the left.

PRACTICE SESSION 18—Mixed Bag

Each sentence below contains an error. Find it; understand it; correct it.

1. "Gridlock" being a word that describes a traffic jam so severe that all traffic comes to a halt. **(12-b)**

2. She hasn't been herself since she opened up the refrigerator and saw some Russian dressing! **(199)**

3. With a simple change of two letters, nuclear physics become UNclear physics! **(23-j)**

4. In the Middle Ages, homeowners took their glass windows with them when they moved to a new house, which proves that glass was scarce at that time. **(30-f)**

5. For an English assignment, me and my friend collected these examples of alliterative place names: Roaring Run, Lovers Leap, Robbers Roost, and Horse Heaven. **(33-b, e.1)**

6. A diplomat is someone who can be disarming even though their country isn't! **(36-c)**

7. Charles Barr says that all a do-it-yourself man needs to quickly make a bay window is a knife and a fork. **(48-a)**

8. They admitted that you getting someone to love you is important—even if you have to do it yourself! **(50-c)**

9. "Jeans" are called "jeans" because the most early purchasers of them were the Italian sailors of Genoa: Genes. **(55-c, 56-c)**

10. Before printing, books were exceeding valuable; for one book written in longhand, the Countess of Anjou paid several skins of costly fur, two hundred sheep, and a load each of wheat, rye, and millet. **(63-d)**

11. She lays in the sun for hours so that she can be the toast of the town! **(159)**

12. One President, Franklin D. Roosevelt, wrote a movie script about the life of John Paul Jones but F. D. R. failed to sell it to Hollywood. **(224-f)**

13. My sister is a born loser: if she bought an automobile stock, someone would try and bring back wagon trains! **(193)**

PRACTICE SESSION 19—Numbers

Which word or phrase in parentheses is correct? (Review #239.)

1. I just read an entire book in (10, ten) seconds—my bankbook!   **(a)**

2. A centipede of southern Europe has over (170, one hundred seventy) pairs of legs.   **(b)**

3. Tourists' Law: No matter where you are, the (1st, first) person you ask for directions will be another tourist!   **(d)**

4. It takes (17, seventeen) muscles to smile, forty-three muscles to frown.   **(a, f)**

5. (14,000, Fourteen thousand) disposable baby diapers are thrown out every sixty seconds.   **(e)**

6. Tennessee is called the Volunteer State because when the government asked for 2,800 men to fight in the Mexican War, Tennessee sent (30,000, thirty thousand)!   **(f)**

7. *Castle Fiend* and *Varney the Vampire* sound like TV shows, but they were actually "penny dreadfuls"—books popular with children in the late (19th, nineteenth) century.   **(g)**

8. The year 2222 should be a lucky year—there will be four ("2's", twos) in its name.   **(h)**

9. On (Eighty-seventh, Eighty-Seventh) Street, the ophthalmologists held their annual shindig—called, of course, an "eye ball"!   **(i)**

10. In 1933 when Chick Reinhart threw a paper plane from a tenth-story office window in Manhattan, it flew (1½, one-and-a-half) miles!   **(j.3)**

11. One lawnmower plus one kid (equal, equals) a mowed lawn; one lawnmower plus two kids (equal, equals) an unmowed lawn!   **(l)**

12. Every week dogs bite (77,000, seventy-seven thousand) people!   **(b)**

13. On (December 6 1960, December 6, 1960,) Betty saw this billboard sign: "Thirty days / hath September / April / June and the / speed offender."   **(g)**

14. An adult's head is (⅙th, one-sixth) the length of its body; a baby's head is (¼th, one-fourth) the length of its body.   **(j)**

15. Silly Suzy said that a ghost residing at (13, Thirteen) Eerie Lane, Merrydale, was arrested for not having a haunting license!   **(g)**

PRACTICE SESSION 20—Mixed Bag

Each sentence below contains an underlined expression. Below each sentence are four possible answers. Which one is correct?

1. My sister the musician she had ought to know that the key to good breeding is "B" natural! **(37-b, 145)**

   a. Correct as is   *c.* had ought
   b. she ought   *d.* ought

2. There are two kind of people who throw parties: the first for the fun of inviting someone, and the second for the fun of *not* inviting someone! **(157, 23-h)**

   a. Correct as is   *c.* to kind of people
   b. two kinds of people   *d.* too kinds of people

3. A cowboy, someone once said, may be defined as parentheses with spurs! **(224-p, 169)**

   a. Correct as is   *c.* said, maybe
   b. said may be   *d.* said maybe

4. Setting on the porch, the old man told me that the first professional baseball game was played in 1846 in Hoboken, New Jersey. **(187, 224-i.2)**

   a. Correct as is   *c.* Sitting on the porch,
   b. Setting on the porch   *d.* Sitting on the porch

5. Our English teacher told we sophmores that we have a strange language: a fat chance and a slim chance mean the same thing! **(37-c, 237)**

   a. Correct as is   *c.* us sophmores
   b. we sophomores   *d.* us sophomores

6. Tom admitted that his sister was more clever than him when she described a squirrel's home as a "nutcracker suite"! **(37-a, 195)**

   a. Correct as is   *c.* then him
   b. then he   *d.* than he

7. A Junior who is at the foot of the class should consider becoming a chiropodist! **(213-c, 30-e)**

   a. Correct as is   *c.* Junior that
   b. junior who   *d.* junior which

PRACTICE SESSION 21—Parallel Structure

Which expression, *a* or *b*, is correct? (Review #20.)

1. If you bite the hand that feeds you, __?__ shouldn't complain of indigestion! **(20-d)**

   a. one   *b.* you

2. Compare the elephants in the zoo with __?__ . **(20-l)**

   a. those in their natural habitat   *b.* their natural habitat

3. *Profiles in Courage* by John F. Kennedy is the only book to make the best-seller list three different times: when it was published, when JFK was elected, and __?__ **(20-b)**

   a. after the President was   *b.* after the assassination of the
   assassinated.   President.

4. She's such a miser that she __?__ down the heat when she lights the candles on a birthday cake! **(20-e)**

   a. turns   *b.* turned

5. "It's more blessed to give than __?__" is the motto of the Internal Revenue Service! **(20-g)**

   a. receiving   *b.* to receive

6. Marriage is like twirling a baton, turning handsprings, or __?__ . It looks easy until you try it. **(20-h)**

   a. to eat with chopsticks   *b.* eating with chopsticks

Be able to correct faulty parallel structure in the following sentences. Parallel items are italicized.

7. He *is* such a reckless driver that a crash helmet *is worn* by the St. Christopher statue in his car! **(20-f)**

8. The fear of women *is called gynephobia*; *androphobia is the name* for the fear of men. **(20-a)**

9. These three prevent most accidents: *courtesy*, *common sense*, and *to be cautious*. **(20-c)**

10. You know it's vacation time when the highway department *closes the regular roads* and *the detours are opened*! **(20-f)**

PRACTICE SESSION 22—Spelling and Confused Words

Test your spelling skill by completing each incomplete word in the sentences below. The three dots (. . .) may represent no letter, one letter, or two or three letters.

1. Unfortunately some people who don't live by princip. . . end up with lots of princip. . .! **(180)**

2. If you have the itch to write, go to the station. . .ry store and get yourself a scratch pad. **(190)**

3. When printed in capit. . .ls, NOON reads the same forward, backward, and upside-down. **(113.3)**

4. A telephone pole never hits a car . . .cept in self-defense! **(77)**

5. Presidents should do well: they get plenty of advi. . .e from the media! **(80)**

6. Despair is to be marooned on a des. . .ert island with a crossword puzzle book and no pencil! **(121)**

7. Some people pay a compl. . .ment as if they expected a receipt. **(116)**

8. Our town may be small, but we have a 50,000-story building—the lib. . .ry! **(238)**

9. In the army of Alexander the Great, all his soldiers had to shave the. . .r. . . faces and heads. **(194)**

10. Gullible Gus kept switching the TV dial until he found a w. . .ther forecast he liked! **(202)**

11. A diplomat is a parent who. . .s. . . two children are on different Little League teams! **(204)**

12. Don't tell jokes about c. . .lings—the punch lines will go over everyone's head! **(234-c)**

13. When a man displays strength of character in his own home, it's called stubborn. . .ess. **(233-a)**

14. What TV gives you is just what you'd expect to get from a vac. . .um tube! **(237)**

15. Firefighter Joe Gregor removed half-baked rolls to answer a fire alarm; lat. . .er he put the rolls back into the oven to finish baking. The result? Brown 'n' Serve Rolls! **(158)**

PRACTICE SESSION 23—Mixed Bag

In each sentence there are three underlined words or phrases. Which *one* of the three contains an error in grammar, spelling, usage, or punctuation?

1. Remember that this life of <u>our's</u> is like a TV talk show: it <u>doesn't</u> <u>always</u> follow the script. **(35-b)**

2. In some of <u>them</u> restaurants you'll see three shakers on every <u>table</u>—salt, pepper, and <u>Alka-Seltzer</u>! **(37-d)**

3. Sign on a <u>government officials</u> door: IT'S DIFFICULT TO SOAR WITH EAGLES WHEN <u>YOU</u> WORK WITH <u>TURKEYS</u>. **(24-a)**

4. Yesterday I read an article <u>where it</u> said that Napoleon used more <u>than</u> fifty bottles of perfume on <u>himself</u> every month! **(75-f)**

5. Some <u>travelers</u> are like cars: they require a large <u>amount</u> of <u>accessories</u>! **(93)**

6. In Norfolk, <u>Virginia,</u> hens <u>can not</u> <u>lay</u> eggs before 8 a.m., or after 4 p.m. **(111)**

7. Said one bachelor: "<u>I could of</u> married any girl I pleased—but I never pleased <u>any</u>!" **(119)**

8. Many receive advice, <u>few</u> profit by it, and even <u>less</u> are <u>grateful</u> for it. **(136)**

9. Before Grover Cleveland became <u>President,</u> he was a sheriff. As sheriff, he <u>personally</u> <u>hung</u> two men. **(146)**

10. <u>Character</u> is what you <u>are;</u> reputation is what you <u>try and make</u> people think you are. **(193)**

11. One student wrote <u>this here</u> brief review of a <u>book:</u> "The covers are too far <u>apart</u>." **(196)**

12. In Chicago, it is illegal to take a <u>French</u> poodle <u>in</u> an <u>opera</u> house. **(151)**

13. After I <u>graduated</u> State College, I learned that the <u>deepest</u> book ever <u>written</u> was Jules Verne's *Twenty Thousand Leagues Under the Sea*! **(144)**

14. <u>Marriage</u> is like <u>an</u> unlabeled can—you <u>have got</u> to take a chance! **(143)**

15. Only a <u>professional</u> skier gets <u>paid</u> <u>good</u> for going downhill. **(141)**

PRACTICE SESSION 24—Agreement of Subject and Verb

From the words in parentheses, select the correct verb form. (Review #47.)

1. Mathematics (help, helps) you to create a budget—and a family quarrel. **(47-c)**

2. Some girls I know (make, makes) up their faces more easily than their minds. **(47-k)**

3. One of the juniors (claim, claims) that a live wire would be dead without connections. **(47-h)**

4. One-fourth of the world's population (live, lives) on less than $200 a year. **(47-o)**

5. Since the late 1960's, the number of people in the U.S. who attend movies (has, have) increased significantly. **(47-p)**

6. A jury (are, is) a group of people who try to decide which contestant has the better lawyer! **(47-q)**

7. In Chicago there (are, is) many eateries punningly named, such as Barnum and Bagel, The Boston Sea Party, and Just Desserts. **(47-s)**

8. Each of the mothers (are, is) strong and square-shouldered—from raising dumbbells. **(29-a, 47-h)**

9. It (was, were) my two aunts who declared that a male is a Boy Scout until he's sixteen and a girl scout thereafter! **(47-r)**

10. Plenty of teenagers (believe, believes) that the atomic bomb is an invention that may end all inventions. **(47-i)**

11. It is either my grandmother or my grandfather who (define, defines) "staying power" as something that visitors have when you want peace and quiet. **(47-f)**

12. My brother and golfing partner (insist, insists) that a golf ball is a golf ball no matter how you "putt" it! **(47-e)**

13. Fran and her friend (describe, describes) an onion as the only thing that can make a cynic shed tears. **(47-d)**

14. Either Harry or his younger brothers (are, is) going to ask the librarian for copies of the 98,721 letters that Lewis Carroll wrote in the last thirty-seven years of his life. **(47-g)**

PRACTICE SESSION 25—Sentence Skills

After each sentence or cluster of sentences below there are several directions. Follow each direction carefully.

1. When the tongue is speeding, it can be safely assumed that the brain is in neutral!
   a. Change "it" to a second person personal pronoun.
   b. Change the verb phrase following "it" to active voice.

2. People have used elephants to fight battles, to build cities, for the transporting of materials, and to carry logs out of forests, which astonished me.
   a. Correct the lack of parallel structure.
   b. The relative pronoun "which" has no antecedent. Rewrite as needed.
   c. Why are commas necessary after "battles," "cities," and "materials"?

3. According to a Georgia district court, love match exist in the imagination of novelist.
   a. Change "match" and "novelist" to plural forms.
   b. Insert the word "only." Should it be placed before "love," before "exist," or after "exist"?

4. When the teacher asked Gullible Gus to define "the prime rate," Gus said it is what his mother cooks when they were having company for dinner.
   a. There is an incorrect shift in tense. Correct it.
   b. Change the last thirteen words into a quotation and add punctuation as needed.

5. He gave digital watches to his two sister-in-laws, capable of giving hourly time signals.
   a. Check all plurals in this sentence. Any wrong?
   b. This sentence contains a misplaced modifier. Rearrange the word order so that the sentence makes sense. Provide any necessary punctuation.

6. Allan and Dave had a conference. He soon learned that there's a difference between letting opportunity knock and knocking opportunity.
   a. Combine into one compound sentence and punctuate correctly.
   b. The pronoun "he" is ambiguous. Provide clarity.

PRACTICE SESSION 26—Mixed Bag

Each sentence below contains an error. Find it; understand it; correct it.

1. It is either Tim or Jim who is so pushy that if they enter a revolving door after you, they still come out ahead! **(36-g.1)**

2. If I (*i*) was in the sun and you (*u*) were out of it, the sun would become—sin! **(46-c.1)**

3. Neither my mother nor my father agree that marriage is a three-ring circus—engagement ring, wedding ring, and suffering. **(47-f)**

4. Give a dandelion a inch, and it will take an yard! **(56-g)**

5. The easiest way to stop a bad habit is to never begin it. **(63-b)**

6. If one wants to know where the sun goes after it sets, stay up all night and it will finally dawn on you! **(20-d)**

7. At a dozen rodeoes, I heard people say that horses staying in a hotel prefer the "bridle" suite. **(23-d)**

8. Their unhappiness is because of illness—they're sick of each other! **(104)**

9. Silly Suzy don't spell accurately, but she makes up for her blunders in originality. **(127)**

10. The biology teacher learned us that the human heart beats more than 100,000 times each day and pumps about 1800 gallons of blood during the same period. **(161)**

11. In 1820 in Maine, the local residents put chains around Cushnoc Island in the Kennebec river and tried to haul it away—with no success! **(211-a)**

12. If he dodges cars, he's a pedestrian, if he dodges taxes, he's a millionaire, if he dodges responsibility, he's a politician. **(222-c)**

13. According to Silly Suzy, a busybody is a person with an "interferiority complex!" **(225-g)**

14. *Mash*, the book that was turned into a long-running TV show, was originally rejected by twenty one publishers. **(239-a)**

15. In the 1930's, people who moved out of Oklahoma and who were poor, unemployed, and didn't have homes were called Oakies. **(20-i)**

PRACTICE SESSION 27—Use of Commas

The following sentences need commas. (The number needed is indicated in brackets.) Where should the commas be inserted? Why? (Review #224.)

1. Cleopatra painted her eyebrows black her upper eyelids blue and her lower eyelids green. [2]   **(224-c.1)**

2. Parents are people who bear infants bore teenagers and board newlyweds! [2]   **(224-b)**

3. A loser is someone who buys a waterproof shockproof and unbreakable watch—and then loses it! [2]   **(224-c.1)**

4. Some people claim that just before an earthquake occurs, dogs act strangely horses stampede pheasants crow and seagulls fly inland. [3]   **(224-d)**

5. When she heard that most of us want to be in the front of the bus in the back of the church and in the middle of the road the foreign visitor decided that Americans are rather odd! [3]   **(224-e, g)**

6. In the twelfth century B.C. China created the first zoo then called a "garden of intelligence." [2]   **(224-h, k)**

7. When giving until it hurts some people discover they are very sensitive to pain! [1]   **(224-i)**

8. Dr. Samuel Johnson to amuse himself in his old age memorized eight hundred lines of Virgil. [2]   **(224-j)**

9. "The thirty-second commercial is also the thirty-second commercial!" complained my brother switching off the TV set. [1]   **(224-k)**

10. Sinclair Lewis who wrote *Main Street* and *Arrowsmith* created Bongo the unicycling bear used in some Walt Disney cartoons. [3]   **(224-l, m)**

11. Golda Meir Prime Minister of Israel in the 1970's spent her childhood in Milwaukee Wisconsin. [3]   **(224-m, q)**

12. The cleric stared hard at the congregation: "And now brothers and sisters let us all give in accordance with what we reported on Income Tax Form 1040." [2]   **(224-n)**

13. When an American tourist said that the inside of the famous volcano looked like hell the guide replied: "Oh you Americans have been everywhere!" [2]   **(224-g, o)**

PRACTICE SESSION 28—Punctuation

What punctuation marks are needed in the following sentences? (The number required is in brackets.)

1. The biggest supplier of food each day is the McDonald fast-food chain the second biggest is the U S Army. [3] **(222-a, 220-b)**

2. When I say that in my neighborhood diamonds are as scarce as hens teeth I mean there are no diamonds at all. [2] **(24-d, 224-g)**

3. "There are three ingredients in the good life learning earning and yearning." (Christopher Morley) [3] **(223-a, 224-a)**

4. There is no such thing as a non-voter if you don't vote you are voting against the thing you would have voted for if you had voted! [2] **(223-b, 224-g)**

5. Ayn Rand the novelist wrote this simile "Polliwogs wriggling in swarms of little black commas." [3] **(224-m, 223-c)**

6. In third-century China kites were used as musical instruments weapons and parachutes. [3] **(224-h, 224-a)**

7. Do you want to avoid criticism Then do nothing say nothing be nothing! [3] **(221-a, 224-d)**

8. Eleven year old Becky Gorton cycled from Olympia Washington to Boston Massachusetts It took her 1½ months. [6] **(230-a, 224-q, 220-a)**

9. There are two finishes for automobiles lacquer and liquor. [1] **(227-d)**

10. We Americans can raise everything skyscrapers bridges and especially taxes and yet too often we don't know how to raise our children! [4] **(227-c, 224-a)**

11. It isnt difficult to meet expenses these days in fact you meet them everywhere! [3] **(226-a, 222-b)**

12. When the instructor said that the appendix is a useless organ a voice from the rear chirped "Not to surgeons! [3] **(224-g, 223-c, 225-a, g)**

13. Poes short story The Murders in the Rue Morgue sold for 12½c in 1843 eighty years later it sold for $25,000! [6] **(226-c, 225-c, 224-m, 222-a)**

PRACTICE SESSION 29—Mixed Bag

In each sentence there are three underlined words or phrases. Which *one* of the three contains an error in grammar, spelling, usage, or punctuation? Why?

1. Several thiefs were talking when one said: "A moment's mistake may result in a lifetime of regret." **(23-f)**

2. Every woman in our luncheon club said that they would agree that a hamburger is a sandwich built from the "ground up." **(36-d)**

3. The octopus, who changes color easily, turns purple when angry. **(30-e)**

4. When one sees a bunch of hoodlums surfing, you can bet the result will be a crime wave! **(37-e)**

5. If a chicken was able to speak, its language—unfortunately—would be foul (fowl)! **(46-c.1)**

6. According to Uncle Tim, mathematics are necessary if you hope to figure out baseball scores and batting averages! **(47-c)**

7. When Silly Suzy visited the seaside, she didn't sleep well because— she said—the ocean snoring kept her awake! **(50-c)**

8. On Brian's report card, a teacher wrote: "Brian may do good at something, but it's nothing we teach here." **(141)**

9. Don't invite a jeweler to dinner without you plan to serve at least fourteen "carrots"! (carats) **(69-b)**

10. In a newspaper ad, I read where a store in the city of San Francisco sells a solid gold mousetrap with diamonds for bait. **(75-f)**

11. Gullible Gus doesn't know much about making bread, but he certainly knows alot about making dough! **(89)**

12. Glenn was mad when the bowling editor rejected his article with this comment: "I'd like to spare your feelings, but this strikes out." **(95)**

13. At our house, opportunity has got to knock; if it phoned, it would get a busy signal! **(143)**

14. Since it is illegal in Dansville, Michigan, to throw spoiled vegetables at an entertainer, can one imply that it is permissible to throw fresh vegetables? **(150)**

PRACTICE SESSION 30—Mixed Bag

Which word in each set of parentheses is correct? Why?

1. My (mother, Mother) (use, used) to insist that a cookbook is a volume that contains many stirring incidents!   **(215-a, 200)**

2. Ernest was so silly he (saved, saved up) (burned out, burned-out) light bulbs for his darkroom!   **(199, 230-a)**

3. She (should have, should of) been a golfer—she (sure, surely) goes around in as little as possible!   **(119, 192)**

4. Printed on her (stationary, stationery) is a Chinese proverb: "I was angered that I had no shoes (until, untill) I met a man who had no feet."   **(190, 237)**

5. My dad is (quiet, quite) the psychologist: he claims that human nature is harder to change (than, then) a thousand dollar bill!   **(182, 195)**

6. "I know a train just (passed, past)," said Gullible Gus. "I can see (its, it's) tracks!"   **(176, 35-c)**

7. The (famous, notorious) Lord Baden-Powell, founder of the (boy scouts, Boy Scouts), could draw two pictures simultaneously, one with each hand.   **(172, 212-b)**

8. How come his (moral, morale) is great even though he (hasnt, hasn't) slept for six days? (Answer: he sleeps at night.)   **(170, 226-a)**

9. Abstract art (may be, maybe) defined as "oodles of (noodles." / noodles".)   **(169, 225-g)**

10. My (freind, friend) brags (as, like) a balloon flies—on hot air! **(234-b, 165)**

11. The money you pay to a babysitter (had ought, ought) to be called (hush money. / "hush money.")   **(145, 225-b)**

12. (Leave, Let) us explore this four-leaf-clover (farm; / farm,) the only one of its kind in the United States.   **(162, 224-m)**

13. The island of Bermuda and the city of Perth, Australia, are (antipodes, / antipodes:) they (lay, lie) on opposite sides of the world.   **(223-b, 159)**

14. In 1969 the first moon walk took place, and a little (later, latter) Pan American (airlines, Airlines) began accepting reservations for commercial flights to the moon.   **(158, 212-a)**

Laugh Your Way Through Grammar

PRACTICE SESSION 31—Sentence Skills

After each sentence or cluster of sentences below there are several directions. Follow each direction carefully.

1. A dog turns around several times before laying down. Because one good turn deserves another!

   a. Is "laying" correct, or should it be "lying"? Why?
   b. Combine the main clause and the sentence fragment into one complex sentence.

2. Michelangelo is the artist who painted the ceiling of the sistine chapel on his back.

   a. Identify the two words that should be capitalized.
   b. The sentence is marred by a misplaced modifier. Rewrite to clarify the meaning.

3. The newlyweds were angry at the best man who pointed out that June, the month for weddings, is followed by fireworks in the month of July.

   a. Something is wrong with "angry at." What? Why?
   b. Make "June" and "July" parallel.
   c. Which sentence is more effective—the original or the one using parallel structure?

4. The Housemakers' Association announced that in they're opinion the best thing to remove black heel marks from off linoleum is toothpaste. It should be applied with a toothbrush (an old one, of course!).

   a. There are two things wrong with the word "they're." What are they? Replace with the correct word.
   b. What error is there in the phrase "from off linoleum"?
   c. Combine the two sentences into one, using a participial phrase to connect the second sentence with the first.

5. She not only suffered from claustrophobia (a fear of closed spaces) but also from acarophobia (a fear of insects).

   a. Correct the "not only . . . but also" construction.
   b. Change the sentence to an interrogative sentence. Make any punctuation changes that may then be necessary.

6. It isn't to hard to believe that the reason a dog has no many freinds is because its tail wags instead of its tongue.

   a. Identify two spelling errors and correct them.
   b. What is wrong with the phrase "is because"? Correct it.

PRACTICE SESSION 32—Mixed Bag

Each sentence below contains an error. Find it; understand it; correct it.

1. Gullible Gus planted razor blades with his potatos—he wanted to grow potato chips! **(23-e)**

2. The two runner-ups in the trivia contest were unable to answer this question: "In whose honor was Minute Tapioca named?" **(23-1)** (Answer: the Minute Men of the American Revolution)

3. It was me who visited the town of Hell in Norway. I wanted to send postcards to my friends: "Wish you were here!" **(33-d)**

4. If anyone insists on wearing a halo, they should remember that if a halo falls a few inches, it becomes a noose! **(36-c)**

5. The Queen Mother of England can play the bongo drums fairly good; she learned the art in 1974. **(141)**

6. Timmy's mother and father was looking for a miracle drug—a medicine Timmy would take without a fight! **(47-d)**

7. It is best to try and fail than not to try and succeed. **(55-b, d)**

8. One thing is always before you, yet you can't never see it—your future! **(63-c)**

9. She spoke so slow that we forgot the beginning of the sentence by the time she reached the end! **(188)**

10. He's different than the other boys she knows: he's willing to go out with her! **(123)**

11. My mother said: "Mrs. Brown is richer than me—her teenager's refrigerator raids are catered!" **(37-a)**

12. When a baby bear was born at our local zoo, the newspaper sent a cub reporter to cover it. **(155)**

13. Any secret you leave your little brother hear goes in one ear and out— to your mother! **(162)**

14. When parents asked why undergraduates had to take on so many English courses, one professor replied: "To teach them a language other than their own! **(69-a)**

15. Some of the people at our table describes the menu as "vittle statistics." **(29-c)**

Laugh Your Way Through Grammar

PRACTICE SESSION 33—Redundancies

A redundant word or phrase exists in each of the following sentences. Identify each; be able to correct the sentence. (Review #240.)

1. The wheel was man's greatest new invention until he got behind it.

2. This clock will never at any time be stolen—the employees are always watching it!

3. Prince Charles hates and loathes golf, the smell of paint, and criticism of George III.

4. It is an unexplained mystery why Elizabeth II always wears horn-rimmed spectacles whenever she wears her crown.

5. On TV news, at 6 p.m. in the evening, one announcer said that litter is our "grossest national product."

6. While studying past history, I learned that the name "Chicago" comes from the Algonquian word meaning "onion-place"—because wild onions once grew in that area.

7. The jeweler, a trained expert with diamonds, announced that an engagement ring is a "buy" product of love.

Which word in each set of parentheses is correct? Why? (Review #47.)

8. Mathematics (help, helps) us to set a budget: a gimmick that tells us what we can't afford but doesn't keep us from buying! **(47-c)**

9. Marty and his sister Mary (claim, claims) they share everything with their parents—especially their homework! **(47-d)**

10. Either Jessie or her friends (call, calls) the gossip research lab a BLABORATORY. **(47-g)**

11. According to one survey, only one of every ten pet-owners (claim, claims) that the pet is unimportant to her or him. **(47-h)**

12. The rest of the alphabet (are, is) unimportant when "U" and "I" get together. **(47-i)**

13. Anyone who reads modern novels (know, knows) that a jacket blurb is a "fable of contents"! **(47-1)**

14. Silly Suzy is one of the sophomores who (think, thinks) that being an astronomer is a heavenly job. **(47-j)**

PRACTICE SESSION 34—Mixed Bag

Which word in each set of parentheses is correct?

1. The artist to (who, whom) I awarded the prize is the one who created this sign for a reducing salon: "A word to the wide is (sufficient, sufficent)." **(37-f.4, 237)**

2. If either of the boys is observant, (he, they) will realize that—unlike McDonald's and Burger King's—(Wendys, Wendy's) hamburgers are square. **(36-b, 24-a)**

3. If I (had wanted, wanted) to play Hamlet in (Shakespeares, Shakespeare's) tragedy *Hamlet*, I would have had to memorize 1,422 lines. **(46-c.2, 24-a)**

4. One of my fellow (juniors, Juniors) (suggest, suggests) that a capital idea is one dreamed up in Washington. **(47-h, 213-c)**

5. Cheese was (originaly, originally) made in the form of a wheel (so, so that) it could be rolled down the mountain to the farm. **(233-a, 75-g)**

6. As an example of atrocious punning, our (history, History) teacher (cited, sighted) this gas station sign: OUR ATTENDANTS ARE FILLING FINE. TANK YOU. **(213-b, 114)**

7. Many (emigrants, immigrants) quickly discover that the (constitution, Constitution) of the United States guarantees free speech but does not guarantee listeners! **(130, 210-c)**

8. (Criticism, Criticizm) is the tax a public official pays for being (eminent, imminent). **(237, 131)**

9. Being a farmer's wife, she (had ought, ought) to know that a farm is a piece of land entirely covered by a (morgage, mortgage). **(145, 237)**

10. Since it was once against the law for frogs to croak after 11 p.m. in Memphis, Tennessee, can one (imply, infer) that many noisy frogs lived there (! / ?) **(150, 221-a)**

11. As he (laid, lay) on the (grass / grass,) Lazy Lou said that he was very good at doing nothing in particular. **(159, 224-g)**

12. The (US / U.S.) will probably (lend, loan) money to Mars if we ever find life on that planet. **(220-b, 163)**

PRACTICE SESSION 35—Mixed Bag

In each sentence there are three underlined words or phrases. Which *one* of the three contains an error in grammar, spelling, usage, or punctuation?

1. Jack told Betty and myself that it's only two syllables from BANK to BANKRUPTCY! **(27-c)**

2. The cavalrymen of Media, which fought the Greeks in the fifth century, went into battle riding ostriches. **(30-e)**

3. It was her who reminded us that when the Lord gave us the Ten Commandments, He didn't mention amendments! **(33-d)**

4. My cousin Lil, as well as the other members of her class, are going to Montana, which was once called the "Stub Toe" state. **(47-k)**

5. According to Jack Smith, the *Los Angeles Times* columnist, three of the beautifulest words in English are "parasol," "larkspur," and "icicle." **(55-c)**

6. What's black and white and exceeding difficult? (Answer: a college board exam!) **(63-d)**

7. When the lawyer told Gullible Gus he had lost his suit, GG replied: "That's alright. I'll buy another." **(91)**

8. When the boss found his accountant kissing the secretary, he asked: "Do I pay you to do this?"
   "No," replied the accountant. "I done it free of charge!" **(126)**

9. To be a skyscraper, a building must have no less than twenty stories. **(136)**

10. Silly Suzy went in the drugstore to have her baby because she had heard the store offered free delivery! **(151)**

11. Harvey is the kind of a person who can remember hundreds of jokes but can't remember to repay one loan! **(156)**

12. My least favorite backseat driver is fond of saying—"Step on it! Don't leave that big truck crowd you off the road!" **(162)**

13. Those kind of people love trivia—for example, that Edward IV of England (1451–83) opened Parliament when he was only three years old. **(197)**

PRACTICE SESSION 36—Confused Words

Which word in parentheses should fill the blank?

1. **(desert, dessert)** At an oasis in the __?__ , a snack bar served apple pie and cheesecake, the favorite __?__s for adults in the U.S. **(121)**

2. **(pray, prey)** In a famine year the bears in the national parks first __?__ for visitors and then __?__ on them! **(179)**

3. **(principal, principle)** It's against her __?__ to pay interest and against her interest to repay __?__ ! **(180)**

4. **(weather, whether)** Even in rainy __?__ , the absent-minded professor wears a wrist compass so that he can tell __?__ he's coming or going! **(202)**

5. **(accept, except)** Do you __?__ the notion that human beings have improved everything __?__ people? **(77)**

6. **(advice, advise)** I feel I should __?__ you that when people can no longer set bad examples, they delight in giving good __?__ ! **(80)**

7. **(all together, altogether)** "Nothing is __?__ wrong," the jeweler told us when we were __?__ in his store. "Even a clock that hasn't worked for years is right twice a day!" **(86)**

8. **(all ready, already)** We were __?__ for a good gossip session when my friend announced that she __?__ knows that her diary is the one confidante that won't reveal her secrets! **(90)**

9. **(anxious, eager)** She was so __?__ to meet the handsome test pilot that she forgot to be __?__ about her pilot's test. **(97)**

10. **(capital, Capitol)** In the rotunda of the __?__ , I heard someone say that __?__ is lending money, while labor is getting it back! **(113)**

11. **(council, counsel)** One member of our town __?__ claims that it is a pleasure to give __?__ , humiliating to receive it, and normal to ignore it! **(120)**

12. **(disinterested, uninterested)** A good judge is always __?__ but never __?__ . **(125)**

13. **(eligible, illegible)** She's __?__ for an award: she paid her doctor with a check with an __?__ signature! **(129)**

PRACTICE SESSION 37—Sentence Combining

Be able to combine each cluster of sentences below into *one* good sentence. The reference numbers suggest possible methods.

1. The sixth President of the United States was John Quincy Adams. Adams won many long-distance swimming races. **(21-a)**

2. In 1694, Queen Mary of England died. King William III, her husband, ordered all members of the court to don black robes—and they've been wearing them ever since. **(21-b, h)**

3. Novelist John O'Hara did all his writing between midnight and dawn. He didn't like interruptions. **(21-c)**

4. Cinderella, West Virginia, was named after a coal company's trademark. The trademark pictured Cinderella sitting before a blazing fire. **(21-d)**

5. The word "plumber" comes from the Latin word "plumbum" which means "lead"—because ancient Romans used lead pipes to transport water. The word "plumbing" comes from the same Latin word. **(21-e)**

6. The beautiful Lillian Russell often donned boxing gloves to spar with famous ring champions. She rode for miles every day on a bicycle with diamond-encrusted handlebars. **(21-f)**

7. A hammer is something you use to hit a nail on the head. You may also use it to hit a nail on your finger! **(21-g)**

8. Everyone knows about Paul Revere's ride. Not everyone knows that Revere billed the Massachusetts State House for expenses for that ride, to the tune of ten pounds four shillings. **(21-h)**

9. The doctor told the Olympic swimmer she had a temperature of 101. The athlete asked thoughtfully: "What's the world record?" **(21-i)**

10. In 1832 Congress commissioned a statue of George Washington to be placed in the Capitol rotunda. The sculptor made Washington shirtless. The public was furious. The statue lurks today in the National Museum of American History. **(21-j)**

11. A ballerina must be graceful and strong. She must have agility, too. **(21-k; see also 20-i)**

PRACTICE SESSION 38—Mixed Bag

In each group of sentences below, the same idea is expressed in three different ways. For *each* group, select the way that is best.

1. (*a*) Queen Elizabeth II thoroughly dislikes dictating letters, laying foundations, and to listen to after-dinner speeches.
   (*b*) Queen Elizabeth II thoroughly dislikes dictating letters, laying foundations, and listening to after-dinner speeches.
   (*c*) Queen Elizabeth II, thoroughly dislikes to dictate letters, laying foundations, and listening to after-dinner speeches.

2. (*a*) A librarian is a person who likes to quickly shelve an idea.
   (*b*) A liberrian is a person who likes to shelve an idea quickly.
   (*c*) A librarian is a person who likes to shelve an idea quickly.

3. (*a*) Inflation is when you do more for a dollar than a dollar does for you.
   (*b*) Inflation results when you do more for a dollar than a dollar does for you.
   (*c*) Inflation is when you do more for a dollar then a dollar does for you.

4. (*a*) When she travels, she favors planes and small compact cars.
   (*b*) When she travels, she favors small compact cars and planes.
   (*c*) When she travels; she favors small compact cars and planes.

5. (*a*) Elections are not only influenced by what the candidate stands for but also by what the voter falls for!
   (*b*) Elections are influenced not only by what the candidate stands for but also what the voter falls for!
   (*c*) Elections are influenced not only by what the candidate stands for but also by what the voter falls for!

6. (*a*) To drink soda from a can, a straw is helpful.
   (*b*) A straw is helpful to drink soda from a can.
   (*c*) To drink soda from a can, you will find a straw is helpful.

7. (*a*) Napoleon I had several nicknames including "The Little Corporal," "Corporal Violet." And "Nightmare of Europe."
   (*b*) Napoleon I had several nicknames including "The Little Corporal," "Corporal Violet"— and "Nightmare of Europe."
   (*c*) Napoleon I had several nicknames. Including "The Little Corporal," "Corporal Violet," and "Nightmare of Europe."

PRACTICE SESSION 39—Mixed Bag

Each of the sentences below contains two (or possibly more) errors. Find them; identify them; correct them.

1. Because in 490 B.C. Pheidippides ran from Marathon to Athens, a distance of twenty-two miles, 1470 yards.

2. A dogwood tree, according to Silly Suzy, is a tree you can recognize easy. By its bark!

3. The world's longest-running play is The Mousetrap by Agatha Christie, it has been playing for over thirty-five years and is still playing.

4. The average women thinks she's a good cook; the average man thinks he's a good driver; the thinking of the average teenager is that someday he or she will be boss.

5. Whom was it, I wonder, who figured out that some fleas accelerate fifty times faster then the space shuttle does after lift-off?

6. Thomas Edison, the inventor, he once said: "When down in the mouth, remember Jonah. He came out alright."

7. What this world needs are pens filled with jelly, not ink, for people whom have to eat their own words!

8. Lowell told me that Richard II (1377–99) had the distinction of being the first british king to use a handkerchief.

9. Not one of the 1,849 Woolworth five-and-dime stores sell anything for a nickle.

10. The bonds of matrimony are like any bonds they take time to mature.

11. The most fastest dinosaur of all should of been called the PRONTO-saurus!

12. The largest African male elephant ever recorded was over twelve foot tall and wieghed about 22,000 pounds.

13. Ludwig Beethoven only wrote one opera: Fidelio.

14. Some men never look up to a woman without they are setting in a bus!

15. When us girls, accompanied by our father, was in South America, we discovered that Argentina is sometimes called "The Land With the Stretched Belt"—because of the large, never-ending dinners!

PRACTICE SESSION 40—Sentence Skills

After each sentence or cluster of sentences below there are several directions. Follow each direction carefully.

1. If one crosses a four leaf clover with poison ivy you will get a rash of good luck!

    a. Correct the lack of parallel structure.
    b. Identify and punctuate the compound adjective.
    c. Provide the one comma needed.

2. During the Mexican War, Ulysses S. Grant acted in an army production of Shakespeare's tragedy, Othello; Grant plays the delicate and beautiful Desdemona.

    a. Correct the lack of parallel structure.
    b. Provide proper punctuation for the title of the play.
    c. Change this compound sentence to a complex sentence and punctuate correctly.

3. Prince Charles passed a whaling ship. He quipped: I bet they're having a whale of a time.

    a. Provide quotation marks as needed.
    b. Change the end punctuation to emphasize Prince Charles' use of a pun.
    c. Combine into one sentence.
    d. Why is "they're" correct rather than "there" or "their"?

4. In 1750 the first cat was imported into Paraguay. It sold for one pound of solid gold!

    a. Combine into one sentence by changing the verb phrase in the first sentence to an infinitive phrase.
    b. Although an exclamation point is not strictly necessary at the end of this sentence, it is preferable to a period. Why?

5. My aunt was a doctor, but she gave it up because she didn't have any patients! My uncle, also a doctor, had the same problem.

    a. Combine the two sentences by using a compound subject.
    b. Change the pronouns so that they correctly agree with the new antecedent.
    c. How would you indicate that the last word of the first original sentence is a pun and has two distinctly different meanings?

PRACTICE SESSION 41—Mixed Bag

Each of the sentences below contains two (or possibly more) errors. Find them; identify them; correct them.

1. We adopt to the circumstances: for example, on April 15, even the most dullest minds make some clever deductions.

2. The sermon had little affect as a single snowflake on an Alpine glacier.

3. All the contestants were aggravated when the critic wrote that an amature show enables people who have no talent to prove it!

4. I agree with the formula that happyness adds and multiplies as we divide it with others.

5. Cattle branding begun in the mid-nineteenth century in Connecticut when farmers were forced to mark all of their pigs.

6. Most all of us are as Columbus: he didn't know where he was going when he started; he didn't know where he was when he got there; and he didn't know where he had been when he got back.

7. The difference among a jeweler and a jailer is that the former sells watches and the later watches cells!

8. Alex felt badly when his wife said he wasn't real bald—he just had an especially large part in his hair!

9. A long time ago, for a month after they were married, newlyweds served honey to any one who visited her home; from that custom, we get the word "honeymoon."

10. The Clairvoyant Society have cancelled its meeting due to unforeseen circumstances.

11. Standing besides a group of Seniors, the guide chanted loudly: "If the Statue of Liberty needed glasses, the frames would have to measure eight feet across."

12. Everyone of the driving students agree that haste makes waste—and dented fenders.

13. A teacher's task is to take a roomfull of live wires and see to it that there grounded.

14. Fishing for complements works good every time—if you use the right bait!

PRACTICE SESSION 42—Pronoun Roundup

Which word in parentheses is correct? Why?

1. The teenager (who, whom) once learned to walk in a year forgets how to do so in an hour—right after receiving a driver's license!

2. The octopus, (which, who) changes color easily, turns purple when angry.

3. (Who, Whom) shall we choose as our club's big-game hunter—a man who can spot a leopard?

4. The other supermarket clerks and (I, me) noticed that yesterday the customers complained about the short weight and today they're complaining about the long wait.

5. Why can't Lenny and (I, me) repeat what Mark Twain said: "A classic is something that everybody wants to have read and nobody wants to read"?

6. It must have been (them, they) who wrote that the best way to eat garlic is—sparingly.

7. When my father told my dog and (I, me) that a porcupine has 30,000 quills and that every quill has 1,000 barbs, Lassie and I decided to stay away from porcupines.

8. In this computer age of (ours, our's), the Eleventh Commandment is— "Thou shalt not fold, spindle, or mutilate."

9. Reserve the apostrophe for (its, it's) proper use and omit it when (its, it's) not needed.

10. No man is brave who—when trouble shows up—thinks with (his, their) feet.

11. You might say of either boy that (he's, they're) so lazy that (he gets, they get) up early in order to have more time to loaf.

12. The debating team mentioned, in (its, their) rebuttal, that Alaska is closer to Russia than it is to any other state in the United States.

13. The only thing Edward can do better than (I, me) is to handle misfortunes—if they're somebody else's!

14. The warden with (who, whom) I was talking said that a reformatory is a place based on the belief that a hitch in time saves nine.

PRACTICE SESSION 43—Mixed Bag

Each of the sentences below contains two (or possibly more) errors. Find them; identify them; correct them.

1. While we were picnicing in the woods, someone said that a dog is like a tree being as they both produce a bark.

2. Our history teacher told we students that the two Presidential candidates are trying to sweep the country with one another!

3. When his brother's-in-law car was stolen, the sociologist blamed everything and every one—except the thief.

4. You can not become a politician without you're a vegetarian—interested in straw votes and grass roots!

5. That there giant clam is broad as a table and can weigh up to 1,000 pounds.

6. In a travel magazine I read where the Scotch word "tartle" is a verb that describes our hesitation when we cannot recall someones name.

7. The best way to forget all of your troubles Virginia is to wear a pair of tight shoes!

8. If you were alive in the sixteenth century and were feeling sadly, you would have said you had the "mubblefubbles."

9. A few spoonsful of magic can make rabbits appear—and tears dissappear!

10. For parents peace comes when all the toys batteries have worn out.

11. U.S. Patent #3,517,423 was taken out for a "carry-all hat"—a hat with a cavity in which the owner could carry jewelery, cosmetics, and even—in some cases—"mad" money is kept there.

12. In England in the eighteenth century, poor people were usualy buried more far from the church altar than were rich people.

13. We have no farther information about whom lies more about their ages—men or women. (According to one study, men do!)

14. We were shocked when the imminent psychologist told us that the only educational television is a television set thats been turned off.

PRACTICE SESSION 44—Verb Roundup

Which word in parentheses is correct? Why?

1. It (was, were) a student who said that the new laundromat is (where, a place where) "grime does pay"!

2. Our biology teacher wants (for us, us) to know that a gathering of quail (are, is) called a covey, and a gathering of geese (are, is) called a gaggle.

3. My sister and traveling companion often (remind, reminds) me that when we (was, were) in L.A., the visibility was so bad that even the birds were walking!

4. When the teacher asked Silly Suzy where the English Channel (is, was), Suzy (shrugs, shrugged). "I don't know," she said. "I can't get it on my TV set."

5. Every morning I (use, used) to read this sign that some wit had (hanged, hung) at a New Jersey intersection: "Cross Road—Better Humor It!"

6. In Maryland there still (are, is) jousting tournaments in which people on horseback (try and, try to) catch rings on their lances.

7. Cats (can, may) be trained: there (are, is) some seeing-eye cats for the blind and some hearing-ear cats for the deaf.

8. If Cleo (had known, knew) you were interested, she would have told you that freckles and pimples (was, were) once called "murfles."

9. After he (emigrated, immigrated) from his native country, the Russian youth told us that a number of pizza parlors in Russia (are, is) now selling red herring pizza.

10. Yesterday Juan almost (burst, bursted) with pride when he heard that in the Old West one-seventh of the cowboys (was, were) Mexican and another one-seventh of the cowboys (was, were) black.

11. Rhoda is one of the women who (believe, believes) that an obstetrician's tax return is clear proof that no one (are, is) born free!

12. Most of the U.S. Presidents (was, were) lawyers before being elected, but neither Harry Truman nor Ronald Reagan (was, were).

13. Neither the boys nor their father (believe, believes) that square meals (make, makes) round people!

PRACTICE SESSION 45—Rewriting

Transform each of the following dialogue jokes into one or two well-written sentences. Experiment with different patterns, with different types of sentence structure.

Example: Cara: Why does your bed keep getting longer?
            Carl: Because two feet are added to it every night!

Rewrites: When Cara asked why his bed was getting longer, Carl replied: "Because two feet are added to it every night!"

            Asked why his bed kept getting longer, Carl retorted: "Because two feet are added to it every night!"

            Cara asked Carl why his bed was getting longer. Carl thought about it for a while, then grinned: "Because every night, two feet are added to it!"

Or even—   Carl's bed keeps getting longer because every night he adds two feet to it!

---

1. Music student: How do I get to Carnegie Hall?
   Piano teacher: By much practice!

2. Visitor: Is the milk in this dairy pasteurized?
   Hired hand: Sure. Every morning we turn the cows out to pasture.

3. Betty: What did you do when your dog chewed on your dictionary?
   Letty: I took the words right out of his mouth!

4. Gullible Gus: How are you taking special care of your new car, Suzy?
   Silly Suzy: I'm being very careful to park it in the safety zone!

5. Jim: How can you find out how many friends you have?
   Tim: Just rent a cottage near the seashore!

6. Kay: Why is Juliet's mind like a blotter?
   May: Because it soaks up everything and then gets it all backwards!

7. Dave: Sally, may I hold your hand?
   Sally: No, thanks. It isn't heavy.

8. Social worker: Now tell me—why did you rob that bank?
   Criminal: Just so I could feel wanted!

PRACTICE SESSION 46—Punctuation Roundup

No punctuation at all has been provided in the following letter. Your task is to provide any punctuation marks needed. You should find about thirty-five.

49 Curiosity Street
Merrydale Idaho 12801
November 14 19_ _

Ms Ellen Dinsmore Reference Librarian
Merrydale Public Library System
123 Biography Boulevard
Merrydale Idaho 12801

Dear Ms Dinsmore

Recently I came across a fascinating anecdote about John Adams our second President Here it is

> Hoping to found an American dynasty Adams tried to marry his son to the daughter of George III George Washington heard about this put on a white uniform and visited Adams trying to talk him out of his plan Washington failed Next GW put on a black uniform and again visited Adams and again he failed Finally GW put on a Revolutionary War uniform and visited Adams for a third time This time he threatened to run Adams through with his sword Adams yielded and our elective form of government was saved

Is this anecdote true Ive checked all the encyclopedia accounts Can you suggest additional sources

I would appreciate any help you can give me Ms Dinsmore since I am writing an article an uncomplimentary one about John Adams personality and would love to include this anecdote but only if it is true Thank you

Very truly yours

Lydia M James

**HOLD IT! The next four Practice Sessions
are a little different. Before proceeding,
read the directions below.**

1. Read the selection once.

2. Read the selection again, this time with pen in hand.

3. Identify—and correct—all the errors you can find. Blunders may be errors of grammar, of confused words, of punctuation or capitalization, even of spelling.

4. If you own this book, underline, circle, cross out, delete . . . as shown in the passage below. If you do not own this book, rewrite each paragraph correctly on separate paper.

Lurking in the wild madness that is Hollywood is Philip Garner, an inventor which is liable to put Rube Goldberg to shame. Garner has a ball inventing the most zaniest things he can think of.

A charming cap designed to be worn by two people simultaneously guarantee togetherness; and Shower in a Can promises respite from dust and heat even if you are lost in the Mojave desert. Sneakers with personalized sole designs leave messages when one runs and high-heel skates encourage you to wildly teeter and totter while you wheel and roll.

Why would anyone spend time on such nonsensical devices? Philip Garner himself has the answer: "to improve, to solve, to simplify, to unencumber." But the answer probably lies in one word—FUN. Garner must have a delightful time dreaming up his delicious concoctions—and an even more delightful time sharing them with others.

PRACTICE SESSION 47—Mastery Exercise

"He stole my thunder"! grumbles one athelete who's victory is dimmed by anothers more greater triumph. The phrase had it's origin in the 18th century.

John Dennis writ plays and for one of these plays he developed a way of banging metal sheets to dramatically simulate the sound of thunder. A few years latter another of his plays were failing dismaly, each night Dennis stares moodily across the street where shakespeares Macbeth was playing to a full house. And each night, during the witching scene, he heard the awesome thunder. Made by *his* metallic sheets. In dispair, he muttered to hisself that they wouldnt let *his* play run, but—they stole my thunder! And so the phrase was born.

PRACTICE SESSION 48—Mastery Exercise

Deep in the heart of New York city only a few steps from honking taxies and irascible citizens is Central Park a charming oasis filled with magnificent trees brilliant flower gardens meandering bicycle paths and scores of small wild animals and deep within Central Park is something no one would never expect to find there a carousel.

What a carousel it is. There are jumpers horses who go up and down on a pole) and standers horses who are stationery). The Central Park horses formally of Coney Island were crafted over seventy years ago but they're manes still fly their nostrils flare their mouths gape wildly from the too tight bits Round and round they go these spirited steeds to the tune of Roll out the barrel.

What better way for any one to welcome spring or to celebrate summer then to joyfully mount a horse insert ones feet in the stirrups and set out for an exuberant circular ride.

Laugh Your Way Through Grammar

PRACTICE SESSION 49—Mastery Exercise

The saintly taxi driver

The best jokes are relevant—related to a current event or situation. Any one who has ever took a taxi ride in New York city Detroit or Los Angeles know the propensity of most all taxi drivers for speed and sudden wild movements. The following joke is based on our' knowledge of this situation.

A catholic priest he died and knocked on the gate of heaven. St Peter answered. "I'm sorry," he said, "But we don't have no rooms left. Perhaps later . . ."

After the priest turned away unhappyly a protestant minister took his turn at heavens gate. He too knocked, and again St. Peter answered. "I'm sorry, but we have no rooms left. Perhaps later . . ."

The minister had barely moved when a jewish rabbi appeared. He, too, knocked at the gate, and he, too, was turned away.

A few minutes latter a taxi driver looking around curiously paused at the gate and knocked. St. Peter greeted him joyfully. "Come right in" he said. "We have a lovely suite waiting for you."

The three clerics feelings were hurt and they rushed back to the gate. "We can not understand this," they chorused. "You have no room for we three who have worked constant all our lives for the cause. We preyed ofen we fasted and we lived in accordance with the highest principals. But for this taxi driver famous for his use of profanity you do have room. How can this be." St. Peter smiled. "My dear friends during his years on earth that taxi driver scared the devil out of more people then did the three of you combined"!

PRACTICE SESSION 50—Mastery Exercise

The case of the mutilated money

Who would put money in a microwave oven, or run it through a washing machine, or hide it in the barrel of a shotgun. The answer is that thousands of Americans do so every year.

For these thousands, there's sometimes a solution. In Washington D.C. a small group of currency sleuths tackle bills that are mutilated, burned, or sometimes someone has torn them and try and reconstruct them. They work on about 40,000 cases annualy and pay out about $14 million. Before they will pay off, however, the government insists that at least fifty percent of a bill be reconstituted—and this isn't easy.

Consider the Iowa farmer who's cow chewed up his wallet and the $600 it contained. After being slaughtered, the stomach and its contents was shipped to Washington. The farmer was lucky; most of the money were pieced together and he received a check for $473.

Another man after hiding several hundred dollars in the barrel of his shotgun forgot about the money and went hunting, when he pulled the trigger his bills turned into confetti. He was able to get back a little of his hoard. But not much.

Some advice: Do not try to dry money in the microwave; it will look well but will disintegrate when touched. Do not bury money deep in the earth; it will solidify into a solid chunk. Do not attempt to "launder" it in a washing machine, or to poach it in a waterbed, or chopping it up in a blender. But if you do, you can send the remains to Washington, wait six months, and—may be—get *some* of your money back.

SECTION II

The Sentence and Its Parts

1. THE PARTS OF SPEECH

Words are classified according to how they are used in a sentence to express a thought. All of them fall into eight groups, called the **parts of speech**. A word may be a . . .

noun:	JIM bought a BOOK about DINOSAURS.
pronoun:	SHE told HER friends that THEY could accompany HER to Europe.
verb:	He WALKS to school when he IS happy.
adjective:	THE BIG, RED apple is BEAUTIFUL.
adverb:	She ran FAST and was QUICKLY tired.
preposition:	IN one minute he ran TO the store FOR milk.
conjunction:	Mary AND Zach are going, BUT Al isn't SINCE he has a previous appointment.
interjection:	HELP! The boat is sinking!

The parts of speech are discussed separately in Section III, ''The Parts of Speech.''

2. THE SENTENCE

A **sentence** is a group of words expressing a complete thought.

It may be very short:

Go.

It may be very long:

> Although he had walked for twenty miles along the dusty country road, he was neither tired nor bored; for he had, with a keen eye, observed the fragile bark of a white birch and the fragile wing of a butterfly and had, with a keen ear, heard the whirr of the cicada and the haunting notes of a pair of loons.

3. SUBJECT AND PREDICATE

All the words in a sentence can be divided into two large groups, the *subject* and the *predicate*.

a. The subject. The subject is the person, place, thing, or idea about which something is said. The subject may be a **noun** or a **pronoun.**

> *Tom* went to school.
> *She* played hopscotch.
> *Paris* is the capital of France.
> *Justice* prevailed.

b. The predicate. The predicate makes a statement about the subject. The chief predicate word is the **verb.**

> Tom *went* . . .
> She *played* . . .
> Paris *is* . . .
> Justice *prevailed* . . .

c. The simple subject and the simple predicate. A sentence may be very short. Nevertheless, to be a sentence, a group of words must have a subject and a predicate.

> Students failed.

In this sentence, *students* (a noun) is the **simple subject,** and *failed* (a verb) is the **simple predicate.**

d. The complete subject and the complete predicate. If the sentence is enlarged, *students* remains the simple subject and *failed* the simple predicate (or verb).

noun   *verb*

Several bright students failed an easy test.

complete subject   *complete predicate*

4. SUBJECT AND VERB (continued)

A sentence contains a *subject* and a *predicate verb* (3).

a. The subject may be a **proper noun.**

> *George Washington* was our first president.
> The *Lincoln Memorial* is beautiful.

b. The subject may be **"understood"**—not stated. Usually the understood subject is *you.*

> Go to school. (*You* is the understood subject.)

c. The subject may be **compound:** that is, made up of two or more subjects connected by a *coordinate conjunction—and, or, but.*

> *Jason* and *Betty* went to the movies.
> The fierce *lion* and the gentle *lamb* are friends.

d. The verb may be **"understood"**—not stated.

> Who broke the window? Nan. (*Did* is understood.)

e. The verb may consist of more than one word, in which case the verb is called a **verb phrase.** A verb phrase contains the principal verb plus one or more **auxiliary,** or **helping, verbs.** Common helping verbs include the following: be, am, is, are, was, were, been; do, did; will, shall, would, should; may, must, might; can, could; has, have, had.

Eddie *wrote* an essay.   (simple verb)
Eddie *will write* an essay.   (verb phrase)
Eddie *has written* many essays.   (verb phrase)

f. The verb may be **compound:** that is, made up of two or more verbs connected by a *coordinate conjunction—and, or, but.*

An elephant cannot *run* or *trot.*

5, 6. PHRASES AND CLAUSES

These sentence parts are often confused although they are significantly different. A *phrase* does not have a subject and a predicate (3), but a *clause* does.

5. A **phrase** is a group of two or more related words conveying a single thought and not having a subject and a predicate. Kinds of phrases are listed below.

verb phrase (4-e):

Someday some smart guy *will throw* a rubber band into the computer and it *will make* snap decisions!

infinitive phrase (48-c):

Said the mechanic: "My advice is *to keep the oil* and *to change the car.*"

participial phrase (49-d):

Grinning mischievously, Larry wrote this brief review of the book he had read: "The covers are too far apart."

gerund phrase (50-b):

Swallowing angry words is better than *choking on an apology.*

prepositional phrase (65):

> An obstetrician may be defined as someone who makes all her
> money *on the stork market.*

6. A **clause** is a group of related words having a subject and a predicate.
There are two kinds of clauses: the *independent* (or *main*) clause and
the *dependent* (or *subordinate*) clause.

$$s \qquad v \qquad\qquad\qquad s \qquad v$$

Everyone applauded the mayor when he promised a bike lane.
     independent clause   *dependent clause*

$$s \qquad v \qquad\qquad s \qquad v$$

Because the roads were icy, the Smiths canceled their visit.
     dependent clause   *independent clause*

a. An **independent clause** has a subject and a predicate and expresses a complete thought. In the above sentences, the subject (*s*)
and the verb (*v*) of each clause are indicated.

b. A **dependent clause** cannot stand alone as a sentence. Although
containing a subject and a verb, it does not express a complete thought.

$$s \qquad v$$

when he promised a bike lane

$$s \qquad v$$

Because the roads were icy

c. Some dependent clauses begin with a *subordinate conjunction* (72-
b). *When, because,* and *although* are common subordinate conjunctions. A subordinate conjunction joins the dependent clause with the
independent clause.

dependent: although the pitcher threw a fast curve
independent: the boy hit the ball

joined: Although the pitcher threw a fast curve, the boy
                   hit the ball.
or: The boy hit the ball although the pitcher threw
                   a fast curve.

Another example:

dependent: when I arrived at the station
independent: the train had already left

joined: When I arrived at the station, the train had already left.
or: The train had already left when I arrived at the station.

d. Some dependent clauses begin with a *relative pronoun* (30). A relative pronoun functions like a subordinate conjunction: it joins the dependent clause with the independent clause to form a complete complex sentence.

dependent: that Jess requested
independent: here is the book
joined: Here is the book that Jess requested.

dependent: who is my sister
independent: Cecilia is a karate expert
joined: Cecilia, who is my sister, is a karate expert.

e. Dependent clauses are used in different ways.

(1) **AS A NOUN** (answers the question ''what'' or ''who'')

noun clause used as subject of a sentence (3-a):

That she is brilliant is obvious.
Where he studied medieval history is uncertain.
                (Notice that a noun clause, however it is used, answers the question ''what'' or ''who.'')

noun clause used as a predicate noun (7-f):

This is *what I require*.
The reason she is ill is *that she doesn't eat properly*.

Laugh Your Way Through Grammar

noun clause used as the direct object (7-b):

Suddenly he remembered *where he had left his bicycle.*
He feared *that his mother would scold him.*

noun clause used as object of a preposition (64-b):

A prize will be given to *whoever wins the contest.*
Pack your suitcase with *whatever you wish to take with you.*

noun clause used as an appositive (17, 18):

The decision *that Mary should be our representative* pleased
  everyone.
We have every hope *that he will rescue us.*

noun clause used as the subject of a sentence beginning with "it"

It is essential *that you attend the conference.*
> (The noun clause is the true subject of *is;* "it" is
> merely an introductory word, an expletive. In subject-
> verb order, the sentence would read: *That you attend
> the conference* is essential.)

    (2) **AS AN ADJECTIVE** (answers the question
  "which one" or "what kind of")

adjective clause modifying a noun or pronoun (30):

The boat *that won the race* belongs to my uncle.
Ellie is the candidate *whom I prefer.*
> (Notice that an adjective clause, like an adjective, an-
> swers the question "which one" or "what kind of.")

    (3) **AS AN ADVERB** (answers the question
  "where," "when," "why," "how," or "to
  what degree")

adverb clause modifying a verb, adjective, or another adverb (57, 58):

> I will clean the house *while you are shopping.*
> Listen carefully *so that you will be able to answer my questions.*
>> (Notice that an adverb clause, like an adverb, answers the question "where," "when," "why," "how," or "to what degree.")

7. COMPLEMENTS

a. As said before, some sentences are complete with only a subject and a verb as its main parts. Examples: "Harry fell." "Several children cried." "The plane landed safely." But some sentences require a third part, a complement. A **complement** is a word that completes the meaning of a verb.

Each sentence illustrated below has a subject and a verb, but the verb does not make a complete statement about the subject . . . until a complement (capitalized) is added.

> For dinner, I had . . . a juicy STEAK.
> (direct object)

> We sent . . . ANITA . . . a Barbie DOLL.
> (indirect object and direct object)

> The winner of the rodeo was . . . ISRAEL.
> (predicate noun)

> Helen is always . . . CHEERFUL.
> (predicate adjective)

b. The **direct object** is the person, place, thing, or idea that receives the action. It answers the question *what* or *whom.*

> The juniors decorated the *gym.*
> d.o.

> Eleanor called *me* yesterday.
> d.o.

c. The **indirect object** is the person or thing "to whom" something is given or "for whom" something is done. It always precedes the direct object. *Easy Aid:* If you have trouble identifying an indirect object, remember that an indirect object does *not* complete a statement. For example, in the following sentence, "Eleanor pitched him" makes little sense until the direct object "strike" is added.

> Eleanor pitched *him* a strike.
>   *i.o.*   *d.o.*

d. An object (direct or indirect) may be a *noun* or *pronoun.* An object (direct) may be a *verbal.*

> Liz called *Michael.*   (a noun)
> Liz called *him.*   (a pronoun)
> Liz enjoys *swimming.*   (a verbal: gerund)
> Liz likes *to swim.*   (a verbal: infinitive)

e. A **compound object** (whether direct or indirect) is made up of two or more objects connected by a *coordinate conjunction—and, or, but.*

> Alison carried a *blanket* and a *thermos* to the game.
>   *d.o.*   *d.o.*
> (compound direct object)

> Their mother gave *Norma* and *Norman* some spaghetti.
>   *i.o.*   *i.o.*   *d.o.*
> (compound indirect object)

f. A *noun, pronoun,* or *adjective* after a **linking verb** (44) redefines or describes the subject. The words lie in the predicate but refer to the subject. (See 3, subject and predicate.)

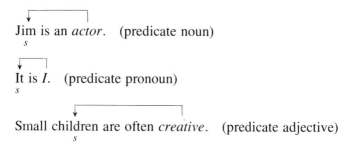

> Jim is an *actor.*   (predicate noun)
> *s*

> It is *I.*   (predicate pronoun)
> *s*

> Small children are often *creative.*   (predicate adjective)
> *s*

8. MODIFIERS

a. A **modifier** is a word that tells something about another word. By providing a specific detail, a modifier *describes* or *limits* the meaning of the modified word.

> She is an *intelligent* girl.
> (tells a *characteristic* of the girl)

> Elsie painted a *red* schoolhouse.
> (tells the *color* of the schoolhouse)

> In baseball, *nine* men take the field.
> (tells the *number* of players)

> *That* fellow is my brother.
> (tells *which one*)

> Ms. Brown selected *Isidore's* com-
> position.
> (tells *whose*)

b. Adjectives and adverbs are modifiers. The italicized modifiers in the sentences above are **adjectives** (52). They tell something about *nouns* or *pronouns*.

Other modifiers, italicized below, are **adverbs** (57). They tell something about *verbs* in the following sentences.

> We will leave for the airport *soon*.
> (tells *when*)

> After school I went *home*.
> (tells *where*; see also 59-b)

> I answered *thoughtfully*.
> (tells *how*; *in what manner*)

> She practices *daily*.
> (tells *how often*)

c. Adjectives and adverbs are classified according to *how they are used in sentences*.

(1) An adjective modifies a noun or pronoun.

> The *pretty* girl won the contest.
>> (modifies the noun *girl*)

> She is *pretty*.
>> (modifies the pronoun *she*; see predicate adjective, 7-f.)

(2) An adverb, most commonly, modifies a verb (57), but it may also modify an adjective or another adverb (58).

> Ron *quickly* sliced the cucumber.
>> (modifies the verb *sliced*)

> Ron is *disturbingly* clever.
>> (modifies the predicate adjective *clever*)

> Ron spoke *almost* brilliantly about skin diving.
>> (modifies the adverb *brilliantly*)

9. TYPES OF SENTENCES

We classify sentences in two ways:

(1) by the way we EXPRESS thoughts (10):
    (declarative, interrogative, imperative, exclamatory)

(2) by the way we STRUCTURE sentences to convey these thoughts (11):
    (simple, compound, complex, compound-complex)

10. DECLARATIVE, INTERROGATIVE, IMPERATIVE, AND EXCLAMATORY SENTENCES

These are the four types of sentences by which we **express** our thoughts: (*a*) the *declarative*, (*b*) the *interrogative*, (*c*) the *imperative*, and (*d*) the *exclamatory*.

a. The **declarative sentence** makes a statement. It ends with a period.

> Candy is sweet.

b. The **interrogative sentence** asks a question. It ends with a question mark.

> Do you like candy**?**

c. The **imperative sentence** gives a command. It ends with a period.

> Beware of the dog.
> Do your homework now**.**

d. The **exclamatory sentence** expresses strong emotion. It ends with an exclamation point. It may be composed of only one word: an *interjection* (76); or it may be composed of several words.

> Help!
> The building is on fire!

11. SIMPLE, COMPOUND, COMPLEX, AND COMPOUND-COMPLEX SENTENCES

These are the four types of sentences according to **structure:** (*a*) the *simple*, (*b*) the *compound*, (*c*) the *complex*, and (*d*) the *compound-complex*.

a. The **simple sentence** consists of one independent clause (6-a). It has one subject and one predicate although either (or both) may be **compound.**

> Archie played football.
>
>> (simple sentence: simple subject and simple predicate)
>
> Archie and Marilyn played football.
>
>> (simple sentence: compound subject and simple predicate)
>
> Archie and Marilyn played football and wrote stories.
>
>> (simple sentence: compound subject and compound predicate)

Note: It would be a mistake to say that, in sentence 3, *Archie* and *Marilyn* are two subjects, or that *played* and *wrote* are two predicates.

b. The **compound sentence** consists of two or more independent clauses connected by a coordinate conjunction. A **comma** is usually placed before the coordinate conjunction in a compound sentence. (The independent clauses are underlined.)

> Dan knew all about fishing, *but* his little brother caught the big one.
>
> An optimist laughs to forget, *but* a pessimist forgets to laugh.

Punctuation Aids

(1) Use a comma followed by a coordinate conjunction to separate the independent clauses.

> Archie played football, *and* Marilyn wrote stories.

(2) Or, use a semicolon (without a comma and without a conjunction) to separate the clauses.

> Archie played football; Marilyn wrote stories.

c. The **complex sentence** consists of one independent clause and one or more dependent clauses (6-b). (The dependent clauses in the examples below are underlined.)

> <u>After she had finished shopping</u>, Nell went to wrestling practice.
>> ("After she had finished shopping" is a dependent clause: it cannot stand alone. "Nell went to wrestling practice" is the independent clause.)

> I never knew <u>what a poor loser I was</u> <u>until I went on a diet!</u>
>> ("What a poor loser I was" is a dependent clause; so is "until I went on a diet." "I never knew" is the independent clause.)

Punctuation Aids

(1) If a *dependent* clause begins a sentence, a comma follows the clause.

> <u>After they had dinner</u>, they went to the theater.

(2) If an *independent* clause begins a sentence, usually no comma follows it.

> They went to the theater <u>after they had dinner</u>.

(3) If a *dependent* clause is located in the middle of a sentence, the clause is usually preceded and followed by a comma.

> My friends, <u>after they had dinner</u>, went to the theater.

d. The **compound-complex sentence** consists of two or more independent clauses and one or more dependent clauses. (The independent clauses in each example below are underlined.)

> If he tries, <u>I will help Jim write his essay</u>, but <u>I will not write it for him.</u>
>> ("If he tries" is a dependent clause; "I . . . essay" and "I . . . him" are independent clauses.)

Keep a ruler on the newspaper as you read it, and you'll get
the story straight!
> ("As . . . it" is a dependent clause; "Keep . . . news-
> paper" and "you'll . . . straight" are independent
> clauses.)

12-16. COMMON SENTENCE STRUCTURE ERRORS

12. Sentence fragment. A sentence that is not complete in itself is called
a **sentence fragment:** (SF). The sentence may lack (*a*) a *subject,* (*b*)
a *predicate,* or (*c*) *both a subject and a predicate.*

a. Wrong: Sent me a bouquet of roses on my birthday.
   (Add a subject.)
   Right: *My brother* sent me a bouquet of roses on my birthday.

b. Wrong: Bobby having a fine scrimshaw collection.
   (Change *having* to a predicate verb.)
   Right: Bobby *has* a fine scrimshaw collection.

c. Wrong: After the game was over and everyone had gone home.
   (Add a subject and a predicate to the dependent
   clause.)
   (1) Right: After the game was over and everyone had gone home,
   the custodians cleared the field.
   (Or change the dependent clause to an independent clause.)
   (2) Right: The game was over, and everyone had gone home.

A fragment may also be (*d*) a *phrase,* (*e*) a *clause,* or (*f*) a *series of
words incorrectly written as if it were a sentence.* As shown below,
the fragment should be attached to the main clause.

d. Wrong: Eternity is paying for a car. On the installment plan.
   (Attach the phrase to the main clause.)
   Right: Eternity is paying for a car *on the installment plan.*

e. Wrong: Football is the cleanest of all sports. Because it's the only
   one with scrub teams.
   (Attach the subordinate clause to the main
   clause.)
   Right: Football is the cleanest of all sports *because it's the only
   one with scrub teams.*

f. Wrong: Love is a word made up of two consonants and two vowels. And two fools.

(Attach the series of words to the main clause.)

Right: Love is a word made up of two consonants and two vowels—*and two fools.*

13. Run-on Sentence. When two sentences are run together without a coordinate conjunction to link the clauses or without a semicolon to separate them, the result is called a **run-on sentence:** ROS.

Wrong: Lazy Lou heard that a particular machine would do half
his work he ordered two!

To correct a run-on sentence, try one of these procedures.

a. Form two sentences. End the first sentence with a period followed
by a capital letter.

Right: Lazy Lou heard that a particular machine would do half
his work. **H**e ordered two!

b. Or form a compound sentence (11-b). Link the clauses with a
comma and a coordinate conjunction.

Right: Lazy Lou heard that a particular machine would do half
his work, **and** he ordered two!

c. Or form a compound sentence by connecting the clauses with a
semicolon.

Right: Lazy Lou heard that a particular machine would do half
his work; he ordered two!

d. Or form a complex sentence (11-c). Study the Punctuation Aids in
11-c.

Right: When Lazy Lou heard that a particular machine would do
half his work, he ordered two!

14. Comma fault. When two sentences are connected by a comma, the result is a **comma fault sentence:** CF.

> Wrong: Golf was once a rich man's sport, now it has millions of poor players.

To correct a comma fault sentence, follow the same procedures as those for correcting run-on sentences (13).

a. Form two sentences. End the first sentence with a period followed by a capital letter.

> Right: Golf was once a rich man's sport. **N**ow it has millions of poor players.

b. Or form a compound sentence (11-b). Link the clauses with a comma and a coordinate conjunction.

> Right: Golf was once a rich man's sport, **but** now it has millions of poor players.

c. Or form a compound sentence by connecting the clauses with a semicolon.

> Right: Golf was once a rich man's sport; now it has millions of poor players.

d. Or form a complex sentence (11-c). Study the Punctuation Aids in 11-c.

> Right: Although golf was once a rich man's sport, now it has millions of poor players.

15. Misplaced modifier. When a modifier is placed incorrectly, a **misplaced modifier** occurs. A modifier should be placed as close as possible to the word it modifies.

a. The position of the modifier should be decided on the basis of logic.

(1) Wrong: Amy selected a dress *in the store* that was made of red silk.

> (Was the store made of red silk? Place the phrase "in the store" at the beginning of the sentence so that "dress" and the clause that describes the dress appear together.)

   Right: *In the store* Amy selected a dress that was made of red silk.

(2) Wrong: We saw a child in the car *wearing a bunny suit*.

> (The car was wearing a bunny suit? Place the phrase "wearing a bunny suit" next to *child*, the noun that the phrase modifies.)

   Right: We saw a child *wearing a bunny suit* in the car.

(3) Wrong: Felix spotted the fire *walking down the street*.

> (A fire can walk? Place the phrase "walking down the street" at the beginning of the sentence, next to the noun *Felix*, which the phrase modifies.)

   Right: *Walking down the street*, Felix spotted the fire.

b. If one noun has a modifier and the other doesn't, place the noun with the modifier second.

(4) Wrong: He enjoys *downhill skiing* and *skating*.

> (Is the skating downhill?)

   Right: He enjoys *skating* and *downhill skiing*.

c. Sometimes moving a misplaced modifier is not enough. It may be necessary to rewrite the sentence or even to create two sentences.

(5) Wrong: Wearing riding boots and safari jackets, the two dogs accompanied their adventurous owners.

> (Were the dogs so clad? Rewrite the sentence.)

   Right: The two dogs accompanied their adventurous owners, who were wearing riding boots and safari jackets.

16. Dangling modifier. When there is nothing in a sentence for a modifier to refer to, a **dangling modifier** occurs.

Wrong: Speeding around the corner, a child was hit.
　　　　　(WHO was speeding around the corner?)
Right: Speeding around the corner, the *car* hit a child.

Wrong: The closet is to the right on entering.
　　　　　(WHO is entering?)
Right: The closet is to the right as *you* enter.
or: On entering, *you* will find the closet is to the right.

Wrong: Strolling down the street, the Washington Monument was a magnificent sight.
　　　　　(WHO was strolling?)
Right: Strolling down the street, *we* found the Washington Monument a magnificent sight.
or: As *we* strolled down the street, the Washington Monument was a magnificent sight.

17-20. VARIATIONS IN SENTENCE STRUCTURE

THE APPOSITIVE

17. An **appositive** is a word, phrase, or clause that tells something about a preceding noun. The appositive explains the noun: (*a*) *defines* it, (*b*) *describes* it, or (*c*) *identifies* it.

a. Jess enjoys using the word gargalesthesia, *the sensation that you get when you're tickled.*

("The sensation . . . tickled" is an appositive, defining *gargalesthesia.*)

b. The mongoose, *a black or brown animal with a long tail*, is being trained to detect drugs at the international airport in Sri Lanka.

("A black . . . tail" is an appositive, describing *mongoose.*)

c. The zoo acquired a boomer, *a male kangaroo*, and a flier, *a female kangaroo*.

> (''A male kangaroo'' is an appositive, identifying *boomer*; and ''a female kangaroo'' is an appositive, identifying *flier*.)

18. A word, phrase, or clause may be in apposition with (*a*) a *subject*, (*b*) a *direct object* (7-b), (*c*) an *indirect object* (7-c), (*d*) or a *predicate noun* (7-f).

a. In 1787, Alexander Hamilton, *the Revolutionary statesman*, described the Constitution as ''a shilly-shally thing of milk and water, which could not last.''

> (in apposition with the subject, *Alexander Hamilton*)

b. Emily operates a ''bawlroom,'' *a nursery for small children*.

> (in apposition with the direct object, *bawlroom*)

c. The doctor gave Emily, *my best friend*, some good news.

> (in apposition with the indirect object, *Emily*)

d. Millie is an egoist, *someone who suffers from ''I'' strain*.

> (in apposition with the predicate noun, *egoist*)

19. PUNCTUATION AIDS

a. If an appositive ends a sentence, it is usually separated from the rest of the sentence by a comma.

> In an emergency he always calls Jeremy**,** *his big brother*.

b. If an appositive is within a sentence, it is usually separated by two commas from the rest of the sentence.

> Jeremy**,** *his big brother***,** is always available in an emergency.

PARALLEL STRUCTURE

20. Parallel structure requires that parallel thoughts be expressed in similar (or parallel) grammatical terms.

a. *Independent Clauses* (6-a):

> Wrong: I washed the dishes, I dried the dishes, and as for putting them away, I did that, too.
>
> Right: *I washed the dishes, I dried the dishes,* and *I put the dishes away.*

b. *Dependent Clauses* (6-b):

> Wrong: I promised Mr. Smith that Ellie would wash the car, the waxing would be done by Jim, and the necessary touch-up work by me.
>
> Right: I promised Mr. Smith *that Ellie would wash the car, that Jim would wax it,* and *that I'd do the necessary touch-up work.*

c. *Nouns* (22):

> Wrong: Jason has big muscles and is very strong.
>
> Right: Jason has big *muscles* and great *strength.*

> Wrong: Lori bought tomatoes, cucumbers, and something to snack on.
>
> Right: Lori bought *tomatoes, cucumbers,* and *snacks.*

d. *Pronouns* (37-e): (unnecessary shift in pronoun)

> Wrong: If one studies, you can pass the test.
>
> Right: If *one* studies, *one* can pass the test.
>
> or: If *you* study, *you* can pass the test.

The Sentence and Its Parts   **75**

e. *Verbs* (40-a): (unnecessary shift in tense)

> Wrong: Pat shook his head, frowned, and moves away.
> Right: Pat *shook* his head, *frowned*, and *moved* away.
> or: Pat *shakes* his head, *frowns*, and *moves* away.

> Wrong: She walked to the store and buys a quart of milk.
> Right: She *walks* to the store and *buys* a quart of milk.
> or: She *walked* to the store and *bought* a quart of milk.

f. *Verbs* (45-c): (unnecessary shift in voice)

> Wrong: Jack did secretarial work, Jill did accounting, and nothing was done by Sally.
> Right: *Jack did* secretarial work, *Jill did* accounting, and *Sally did* nothing.

g. *Infinitives* (48-a):

> Wrong: He likes to swim, go boating, and surfing.
> Right: He likes *to swim*, *to boat*, and *to surf*.
> or: He likes *to swim*, *boat*, and *surf*.

h. *Gerunds* (50-a):

> Wrong: He likes swimming and to go boating and surfing.
> Right: He likes *swimming*, *boating*, and *surfing*.

i. *Adjectives* (52):

> Wrong: Merrilee is tall and has strength.
> Right: Merrilee is *tall* and *strong*.

j. *Prepositional Phrases* (65):

> Wrong: Gertrude, a little kangaroo, is a trademark used in some paperbacks and advertisements.
> Right: Gertrude, a little kangaroo, is a trademark used *in some paperbacks* and *in some advertisements*.

k. *Correlatives* (certain coordinating conjunctions) (73): Notice that the grammatical construction after EACH conjunction is parallel.

> Wrong: He gave gifts BOTH to his hostess AND her sister.
> Right: He gave gifts BOTH *to his hostess* AND *to her sister.*
> or: He gave gifts to BOTH *his hostess* AND *her sister.*

> Wrong: This money is EITHER for you OR your sister.
> Right: This money is EITHER *for you* OR *for your sister.*
> or: This money is for EITHER *you* OR *your sister.*

l. *Incomplete Parallel Structure:* Be sure to include all the words necessary to make parallel structure complete. An omission can cause incomplete parallel structure *and* make the meaning unclear.

> Wrong: Compare the books in the study with the garage.
> (Compare "books" with "garage"? Surely not!)
> Right: Compare the books *in the study* with those *in the garage.*

> Wrong: Dogs chase cats more often than people.
> Right: *Dogs chase cats* more often than *they chase people.*
> or: *Dogs chase cats* more often than *people do.*

21. SENTENCE COMBINING: A SUMMARY OF SENTENCE STRUCTURE VARIATIONS

Sentence combining can turn two or three short, choppy sentences into one smooth, rhythmical sentence. There are a number of procedures for doing this.

a. Combine by constructing an APPOSITIVE (17).

> Choppy: Clara Barton founded the American Red Cross. At one time, she wanted to be a soldier.
> Smooth: Clara Barton, *the founder of the American Red Cross,* at one time wanted to be a soldier.

b. Combine by constructing a PREPOSITIONAL PHRASE (65).

> Choppy: Lee went to the store. He wanted to buy two video-
> tapes and a tape eraser.
> Smooth: Lee went to the store *for two videotapes and a tape
> eraser.*

c. Combine by constructing an INFINITIVE PHRASE (48-c).

> Choppy: Lee went to the store. He wanted to buy two video-
> tapes and a tape eraser.
> Smooth: Lee went to the store *to buy two videotapes and a
> tape eraser.*

d. Combine by constructing a PARTICIPIAL PHRASE (49-d).

> Choppy: Tim set off for a day of hiking. He was whistling
> merrily.
> Smooth: *Whistling merrily,* Tim set off for a day of hiking.

e. Combine by constructing a COMPOUND SUBJECT (4-c), using
a coordinate conjunction to join the subjects.

> Choppy: Human beings flirt. Birds flirt, too.
> Smooth: *Human beings* AND *birds* flirt.

> Choppy: At birth, baby chicks recognize the silhouette of a
> hawk. So do ducklings. So do goslings.
> Smooth: At birth, *baby chicks, ducklings,* AND *goslings* rec-
> ognize the silhouette of a hawk.

f. Combine by constructing a COMPOUND VERB (4-f), using a coordinate conjunction to join the verbs.

> Choppy: Zoo animals that need a vacation slink into hideaways. They sulk.
> Smooth: Zoo animals that need a vacation *slink* into hideaways AND *sulk.*

> Choppy: Thornton Wilder's *Our Town* made its debut in 1938. It has been performed somewhere every day since.
> Smooth: Thornton Wilder's *Our Town made* its debut in 1938 AND *has been performed* somewhere every day since.

g. Combine by constructing a COMPOUND OBJECT (7-e), using a coordinate conjunction to join the objects.

> Choppy: In a poll, British children said they disliked snakes. They also disliked spiders.
> Smooth: In a poll, British children said they disliked *snakes* AND *spiders.* (compound direct object)

> Choppy: Aaron told me that Henry II (1154–1189) was the first English king to read a book in bed. He told my brother, too.
> Smooth: Aaron told my *brother* AND *me* that Henry II (1154–1189) was the first English king to read a book in bed. (compound indirect object)

h. Combine by constructing a COMPOUND SENTENCE (11-b), using a coordinate conjunction or a semicolon (222-a) to join the clauses.

> Choppy: We make a living by what we get. We make a life by what we give.
> Smooth: We make a living by what we get, BUT we make a life by what we give.
> Smooth: We make a living by what we get; we make a life by what we give.

i. Combine by constructing a COMPLEX SENTENCE (11-c), using a subordinate conjunction to form a dependent clause.

> Choppy: The tramp asked for something to eat. The farmer suggested that he go to the woodshed and take a few chops.
>
> Smooth: *When the tramp asked for something to eat*, the farmer suggested that he go to the woodshed and take a few chops.

j. Combine by constructing a COMPOUND-COMPLEX SENTENCE (11-d).

> Choppy: Corinne is an intelligent girl. She is studying hard. She hopes to win the scholarship
>
> First, construct a compound sentence (21-h).
>
> Smooth: Corinne is an intelligent girl, AND she is studying hard.
>
> Then use a subordinate conjunction to form a dependent clause, and attach the dependent clause to the compound sentence.
>
> Smooth: Corinne is an intelligent girl, AND she is studying hard BECAUSE she hopes to win the scholarship.

k. Combine by using PARALLEL STRUCTURE (20).

> Choppy: George likes cats. He also likes dogs. He likes hamsters, too.
>
> Smooth: George likes cats, dogs, and hamsters.

> Choppy: Georgina hits home runs. She throws spectacular passes. She putts with deadly accuracy.
>
> Smooth: Georgina hits home runs, throws spectacular passes, and putts with deadly accuracy.

l. Combine by using a SEMICOLON (222-a).

> Choppy: My mother and father do everything together. They even got married at the same time.
>
> Smooth: My mother and father do everything together; they even got married at the same time.

SECTION III
The Parts of Speech

NOUNS

Continued on Following Page

ADJECTIVES

NOUNS

22. A NAME WORD: THE NOUN

A **noun** is the name of a person, place, thing, or event. All nouns are classified as either (*a*) *common* or (*b*) *proper*.

a. A **common noun** names *any one* of a class or group of persons, places, things, or events. A **proper noun** names a *particular* person, place, thing, or event.

	COMMON NOUN	PROPER NOUN
person:	boy	Tom
place:	state	Nebraska
thing:	car	Ford
event:	war	Revolutionary War

b. A common noun is never capitalized; a proper noun is always capitalized. (For a further study of the capitalization of proper nouns, see 210.)

NOT CAPITALIZED	CAPITALIZED
boy	Tom Brown
canyon	Grand Canyon
street	First Street

c. A **compound noun** is made up of two or more words.

mother-in-law	Miami Beach
firefighter	Washington, D.C.
commander in chief	Secretary of State

d. A **collective noun** names a group.

team	class	army
audience	jury	committee

23. SINGULAR AND PLURAL OF NOUNS

A noun may be **singular** (*one*) or **plural** (*more than one*) in number. (In grammar, *number* means the form of a word to show whether one or more than one is meant.) To form the plural of most nouns, just add an **s**.

dog—dog**s**	house—house**s**
toy—toy**s**	tray—tray**s**

a. If a singular noun ends in **ch**, **sh**, **s**, **x**, or **z**, add **es**.

church—church**es**	box—box**es**
bush—bush**es**	topaz—topaz**es**
guess—guess**es**	

b. If a singular noun ends in **y** and the **y** is preceded by a consonant, change the **y** to **i** and add **es**.

baby—bab**ies**	fly—fl**ies**
lady—lad**ies**	sky—sk**ies**

However, do *not* follow this rule with proper nouns. You may talk about three "Mar**ys**" or the "Kell**ys**."

c. If a singular noun ends in **y** and the **y** is preceded by a vowel, keep the **y** and add **s**. (The *vowels* are *a, e, i, o, u*. All the other letters of the alphabet are *consonants*.)

jockey—jockey**s**	turkey—turkey**s**
monkey—monkey**s**	day—day**s**

d. If a singular noun ends in **o** and the **o** is preceded by a vowel, add **s**.

radio—radio**s**	curio—curio**s**
trio—trio**s**	patio—patio**s**

e. (1) If a singular noun ends in **o** and the **o** is preceded by a consonant, add **es**.

tomato—tomato**es**   potato—potato**es**   veto—veto**es**

(2) However, other words of this type form the plural by simply adding **s**.

piano—piano**s**   photo—photo**s**   radio—radio**s**
disco—disco**s**   solo—solo**s**   dynamo—dynamo**s**

(3) Still other words of this type form the plural by adding **s** OR **es**. (If you are uncertain, consult a dictionary.)

volcano—volcano**s** or volcano**es**
tornado—tornado**s** or tornado**es**

f. If a singular noun ends in **f** or **fe**, sometimes, to form the plural, change the **f** or **fe** to **v** and add **es**.

elf—el**ves**   leaf—lea**ves**   shelf—shel**ves**
half—hal**ves**   life—li**ves**   thief—thie**ves**
hoof—hoo**ves**   loaf—loa**ves**   wife—wi**ves**
knife—kni**ves**   self—sel**ves**   wolf—wol**ves**

However, other **f** and **fe** words form the plural by simply adding **s**. (One way to be sure of the correct spelling of **f** and **fe** words is to memorize them! Another way is to consult a dictionary.)

belief—belief**s**   cliff—cliff**s**   roof—roof**s**
chief—chief**s**   proof—proof**s**   safe—safe**s**

g. Some nouns form the plural by adding **en** or **ren**: ox—ox**en**; child—child**ren**.

h. Some nouns form the plural by changing, adding, or deleting a vowel within the word.

man—**men**   louse—**lice**   goose—**geese**
mouse—**mice**   woman—**women**   tooth—**teeth**

The Parts of Speech   **85**

i. Some nouns have the same form, regardless of number.

deer—deer	sheep—sheep
series—series	moose—moose

j. Some nouns look plural but are actually singular. (Also see 47-c.)

measles	ethics
mumps	economics

Right: *Economics is* a required course in our school.

k. Some nouns are always plural, never singular.

trousers	scissors
tongs	clothes

l. Compound words usually form the plural by adding **s** to the main part of the word.

mother-in-law	mother**s**-in-law
Board of Education	Board**s** of Education
passerby	passer**s**by

m. A singular noun ending in **ful** forms the plural by adding **s** at the end of the word.

spoonful	spoonful**s**
cupful	cupful**s**

n. Letters, numbers, and occasionally words form the plural by adding **'s.**

There are three ''2's'' in the example.
There are two ''n's'' in the word ''dinner.''

o. A noun borrowed from a foreign language often retains its foreign plural.

SINGULAR	PLURAL
datum	data
phenomenon	phenomena
alumna	alumnae
alumnus	alumni

24. POSSESSIVE CASE OF NOUNS

The **possessive case** is used to show *ownership* or *possession*.

a. Singular possession: If a singular noun does not end in **s**, add an apostrophe and **s** (**'s**).

SINGULAR NOUN	POSSESSIVE CASE
Mary	Mary**'s** coat
girl	girl**'s** essay
clown	clown**'s** painted face
giraffe	giraffe**'s** neck
book	book**'s** cover

b. If the singular form of a noun ends in **s**, add only an apostrophe instead of **'s** to avoid the awkwardness of the additional **s** sound.

Jesus	for Jesus' sake
class	our class' record

c. Plural possession: The above rules also apply for forming the possessive case of plural nouns. Hint: first write the plural form of the noun. If the plural noun does not end in **s**, add **'s**.

PLURAL NOUN	POSSESSIVE CASE
men	men**'s** clothing
women	women**'s** movement
children	children**'s** toys

d. If the plural noun ends in **s**, add only an apostrophe.

boys	boys' coats
girls	girls' boots
officers	officers' orders

e. A compound noun forms the possessive by adding an apostrophe or an **'s** to the last word.

SINGULAR NOUN	POSSESSIVE CASE
sister-in-law	sister-in-law**'s** house
Secretary of State	Secretary of State**'s** message
United Nations	United Nations' policy

f. If two nouns own the same thing, the apostrophe or **'s** is added to the second noun.

Tom and Dick**'s** dog (both own the same dog)

If each noun owns something individually, the sign of possession is placed after each noun.

Tom**'s** and Dick**'s** feet (each boy has his own feet)

g. If a noun precedes a gerund (a verbal noun ending in *ing*), the noun is usually in the possessive case.

The audience applauded David**'s** singing of the national anthem.

PRONOUNS

25. A NOUN SUBSTITUTE: THE PRONOUN

a. A **pronoun** is a word that takes the place of a *noun*. By substituting a pronoun for a repeated noun, you produce a smoother sentence.

> Awkward: Tim's very orderly. *Tim* even eats *Tim's* alphabet soup alphabetically!
>
> Smooth: Tim's very orderly. *He* even eats *his* alphabet soup alphabetically!

> Awkward: Writers are the strangest people: *writers'* tales come out of *writers'* heads!
>
> Smooth: Writers are the strangest people: *their* tales come out of *their* heads!

b. Pronouns cause trouble because they change their form according to how they are used in sentences. For example, *I* changes to *me* and *my* in the following sentences.

> *I* called Frank.
> Frank visited *me*.
> He is *my* cousin.

c. The study of pronouns is further complicated by the large number of pronouns in our language and the many groups into which they have been classified.

> personal pronouns (26)
> compound personal pronouns (27)
> demonstrative pronouns (28)
> indefinite pronouns (29)
> relative pronouns (30)
> interrogative pronouns (31)

26–31. KINDS OF PRONOUNS

26. Personal pronouns refer to *persons*. Certain personal pronouns distinguish the speaker (first person), or the person spoken to (second person), or the person, place, or thing spoken about (third person).

> **First person:** I, my, mine, me, we, our, ours, us
>
> **Second person:** you, your, yours
>
> **Third person:** he, she, it, his, her, hers, its,
> him, they, their, theirs, them

> Note: *it (its)* is the only personal pronoun that does not refer to persons.

27. A **compound personal pronoun** is formed by adding the suffix *self* or *selves* to the simple pronoun.

SINGULAR	PLURAL
her—herself	them—themselves
him—himself	your—yourselves
my—myself	our—ourselves

> (But NEVER "hisself" or "theirselves.")

a. A compound personal pronoun may be **intensive:** used to show emphasis.

> He *himself* is guilty.

b. A compound personal pronoun may be **reflexive:** used to refer to the subject.

> She voted for *herself*. (she = herself)

> Eric dressed *himself*. (Eric = himself)

c. Unless the pronoun has a clear antecedent, as in the preceding examples, the compound form should not be substituted for the simple form.

> Wrong: The only exercise my sister and *myself* get is running up bills.
>
> Right: The only exercise my sister and *I* get is running up bills.

28. A **demonstrative pronoun** points out a person, place, or thing.

a. The most common demonstrative pronouns are *this*, *that*, *these*, and *those*.

SINGULAR	PLURAL
This is my VCR.	*These* are my VCR tapes.
That is my VCR.	*Those* are my VCR tapes.

b. *This* and *these* = nearby. *That* and *those* = farther away.

29. An **indefinite pronoun** refers *indefinitely* to a person, place, or thing.

a. Some indefinite pronouns are always SINGULAR.

another	each	everything	nothing
anybody	either	neither	one
anyone	everybody	nobody	somebody
anything	everyone	no one	someone

> Right: *Neither is* my sister.
> Right: *Everyone* in my class *has* a new book.

b. Some indefinite pronouns are always PLURAL: *both*, *few*, *many*, *several*.

> Right: "*Many are* called, but *few are* chosen."
> Right: *Several* of the girls *have* been selected for camp.

c. Some indefinite pronouns are sometimes singular, sometimes plural.

ANY: *Is* any *of the applesauce* left? (singular)
Are any *of the apples* ripe? (plural)

> Notice: The phrase that follows the indefinite pronoun affects its number.
> "Applesauce" is a mass: it can't be counted. (Other examples: spinach, grass, cereal.)
> "Apples" are individuals: they can be counted. (Other examples: dollars, books, potatoes.)

MOST: Most of the applesauce *has* been eaten. (singular)
Most of the apples *have* been eaten. (plural)

NONE: None of the applesauce *is* left. (singular)
None of the apples *are* left. (plural)

SOME: Some of the applesauce *has* been eaten. (singular)
Some of the apples *have* been eaten. (plural)

30. A **relative pronoun** introduces a dependent clause and joins the clause to a related word (its antecedent). Common relative pronouns are *who*, *that*, *which*, and *what*. (Dependent clauses are underlined.)

a. The following dependent clauses modify a noun and are called *adjective clauses*.

We prayed for the child who fell into the well.

Helen ordered chocolate, which is not on her diet.

I found the sweater (that) you lost.
> (Sometimes the relative pronoun may be omitted, as in this sentence.)

b. The relative pronouns *that*, *which*, and *what* have the same form in the nominative and objective cases. *Who*, however, changes form.

> People *who* eat sweets take up two seats!
> (*Who*, nominative case, is subject of *eat*.)

> He is the candidate for *whom* I voted.
> (*Whom*, objective case, is object of the preposition *for*.)

> The woman *whose* trouble is all behind her is probably a school bus driver!
> (*Whose* is the possessive case.)

c. The suffix *ever* when added to *who*, *whom*, *which*, and *what* forms the **compound relative pronouns** *whoever*, *whomever*, *whichever*, and *whatever*.

d. A relative pronoun functions as subject or object in its own clause. (See 37-f.)

> (1) The student who ran the campaign is Fred Smith.
>
> (*Who* is subject of the verb *ran*.)

> (2) The student whom I selected is Fred Smith.
>
> (*Whom* is object of the verb *selected*.)

e. The relative pronoun *who* is always used to refer to persons; *which* to animals or things; and *that* to either persons, places, or things. (See also item 203.)

f. *Which* should NEVER be used to refer to a complete clause.

> Wrong: She was absent, *which* caused her to fail the test.
>
> Right: It was her absence *which* caused her to fail the test.
>
> or: She was absent and therefore failed the test.
>
> or: Her absence caused her to fail the test.
>
> or: She failed the test because she was absent.

31. An **interrogative pronoun** is used to ask a question. The interrogative pronouns are *who (whom, whose)*, *which*, and *what*.

> *Whose* is this?
> *Which* do you prefer?
> *What* shall we do?

The case of *who, whom* depends on the way it is used in a sentence.

> *Who* is going to the party? (subject of the verb *is going*)
> *Who* do you suppose is going to the party? (The interrupter *do you suppose* does not affect the subject–verb agreement of *Who is going*.)
> *Whom* shall we invite? (object of the verb *shall invite*)
> To *whom* did you give the book? (object of the preposition *to*)

Easy Aid: If you are uncertain as to whether to use *who* or *whom* in a sentence, change the question to a statement.

> Question: (*Who, Whom*) is going to the party?
> Answer: *She* is going to the party. (*She* is nominative case, so *who* is correct.)

> Question: (*Who, Whom*) shall we invite?
> Answer: We shall invite *her*. (*Her* is objective case, so *whom* is correct.)

> Question: To (*who, whom*) did you give the book?
> Answer: You gave the book to *him*. (*Him* is objective case, so *whom* is correct.)

32–35. CASE

32. The term **case** is used to explain the relation of a noun or pronoun to the other words in a sentence. There are three cases: *nominative, objective, possessive.*

a. The form of a noun does not change to indicate case, except for the possessive. But the form of a personal pronoun does change according to its use in a sentence.

	NOUN	PRONOUN
nominative:	The *boy* was lost.	*He* was lost.
objective:	Bill found the *boy.*	Bill found *him.*
possessive:	The *boy's* parents were alarmed.	*His* parents were alarmed.

b. Study the nominative and objective forms of the personal pronouns.

	NOMINATIVE		OBJECTIVE	
	SINGULAR	PLURAL	SINGULAR	PLURAL
1st person:	I	we	me	us
2nd person:	you	you	you	you
3rd person:	he		him	
	she	they	her	them
	it		it	

33. **a.** The **nominative case** is used when the pronoun is the *subject* of a verb.

   (1) *She* received an "A" in her favorite subject—BUY-ology!
       (*She* is subject of the sentence.)

   (2) *I* studied French, and *she* took Spanish.
       (*I* and *she* are subjects of the independent clauses.)

   (3) Rob will visit the Grand Canyon next summer if *he* saves enough money.
       (*He* is subject of the dependent clause "if . . . money.")

   b. Observe the same rule even when the subject is *compound.* (See also *e* of this section.)

   Liz and *I* are going to the skating rink. ("I and Liz" would also be correct, but "Liz and I" is preferred.)
   He and *Maria* never tell a secret to the rich because money talks!

   (*continued*)

The Parts of Speech

Easy Aid: If you have trouble with the preceding rule, try the elimination trick. For example: (He? Him?) and Maria never tell a secret. Eliminate "and Maria." You would say "He never tells a secret," wouldn't you?

c. In an interrogative sentence, change the question to a statement.

> Did (*she, her*) and Frank get married?
> (*She, her*) and Frank did get married.
> (Now it is clear that *she*, the subject, is correct.)

d. A predicate pronoun (7-f) takes the nominative case. A predicate pronoun follows any form of the verb *be*: am, is, are, was, were, been.

> It was *I* who said that finding a doctor today is a matter of course—the golf course! (*It = I.*)
> The expert who told us that a steel ball will bounce higher than a rubber ball was *he*. (*Expert = he*)

The verb *be* functions not only as an *auxiliary verb* (4-e) but also as a *linking verb* (44) because it connects the subject with the predicate pronoun.

e. Avoid these common errors in case:

Use the *nominative* case when the subject is compound.

> (1) Wrong: *You* and *me* know that smiles are just like colds—they're catching!
>
> (You wouldn't say: *Me* know that . . .)
>
> Right: *You* and *I* know that smiles are just like colds—they're catching!
>
> (2) Wrong: We found courage when *him* and *me* heard that triumph is just "umph" added to "try."
>
> (You wouldn't say: *Him* heard that . . . or *Me* heard that . . .)
>
> Right: We found courage when *he* and *I* heard that triumph is just "umph" added to "try."

Use the *nominative* case when the predicate pronoun is compound.

    (3) Wrong: The guilty parties are *him* and *me*.
        Right: The guilty parties are *he* and *I*.

    (4) Wrong: Was it *you* or *her* who said that an accountant is
               merely a figurehead?
        Right: Was it *you* or *she* who said that an accountant is
               merely a figurehead?

34. a. The **objective case** is used when the pronoun is the *direct object* of a verb (7-b).

> The class bully hit *him*.
> The announcer introduced *them*.
> The monkey slapped *Jim* and *me*.
>
> > (compound direct object. You wouldn't say: The monkey slapped *I*.)

b. The objective case is used when the pronoun is the *indirect object* (7-c).

> His mother gave *him* a dollar.
> The messenger brought *her* a telegram.
> The monkey gave *Jim* and *me* its banana.
>
> > (compound indirect object. You wouldn't say: The monkey gave *I* its banana.)

c. The objective case is used when the pronoun is the *object of a preposition* (64).

> According to *him*, a person who knows everything has a lot to learn.
> Barbara saved some spaghetti for *them*.
> The monkey shared its banana with *Jim* and *me*.
>
> > (compound object of a preposition. You wouldn't say: The monkey shared its banana with *I*.)

d. Avoid these common errors in case:

Use the *objective* case when the object is compound.

(1) Wrong: Our teacher congratulated *Tess* and *I* when we
defined "comet" as a long-haired star.
Right: Our teacher congratulated *Tess* and *me* when we
defined "comet" as a long-haired star.
(compound direct object)

(2) Wrong: Their employer gave *she* and *Ben* a day off before the Thanksgiving holiday.
Right: Their employer gave *her* and *Ben* a day off before the Thanksgiving holiday.
(compound indirect object)

(3) Wrong: Mother agreed with *Vic* and *I* when we said that
a donkey is beautiful to a donkey and a pig to a
pig.
Right: Mother agreed with *Vic* and *me* when we said
that a donkey is beautiful to a donkey and a pig
to a pig.
(compound object of a preposition)

35. a. The **possessive case** is used to show *ownership* or *possession*. The possessive form of a noun (24) contains either an apostrophe alone or an apostrophe and **s** (Jack**'s** coat, Bess' shoes).

b. The possessive case of a personal pronoun, on the other hand, NEVER includes an apostrophe (*hers*, not her's; *yours*, not your's; *ours*, not our's; *theirs*, not their's). The possessive case of some indefinite pronouns, however, does require an apostrophe (*one's, anyone's, someone's*).

c. When *it's* contains an apostrophe, it is a contraction meaning "it is." The possessive of *it* is *its*.

Imitation is the sincerest form of flattery—except when *it's* forgery. (contraction)

The owl can swivel *its* head and look directly backwards. (possessive)

Laugh Your Way Through Grammar

d. These are the possessive case forms.

	SINGULAR	PLURAL
1st person:	my, mine	our, ours
2nd person:	your, yours	your, yours
3rd person:	his	
	her, hers }	their, theirs
	its	

Some of these pronouns—*my, your, his, her, its, our, their*—are modifiers of nouns, as in 36-a below. Although they are pronouns, they act as adjectives, called *possessive adjectives*.

36. AGREEMENT OF PRONOUN AND ANTECEDENT

a. The **antecedent** of a pronoun is the word to which the pronoun refers. The pronoun must agree with its antecedent in *gender* and *number*.

Right: Lucy asked for *her* allowance.

(*Lucy*, the antecedent of *her*, is singular and feminine. So the singular, feminine pronoun *her* is correct.)

Right: They take good care of *their* dogs.

(*They*, the antecedent of *their*, is plural and of common gender—that is, including masculine and feminine. So the plural, common gender pronoun *their* is correct.)

b. Use a singular pronoun to refer to a singular *indefinite pronoun* (29-a).

Right: *Neither* of the boys is going to drive *his* car.

(*Neither* is singular, so the singular pronoun *his* is correct.)

If the indefinite pronoun is plural (29-b), use a plural pronoun.

Right: *Many* are going to drive *their* cars.

(*Many* is plural, so the plural pronoun *their* is correct.)

c. Singular indefinite pronouns (29-a), such as *everyone, somebody*, and *everybody*, may include males and females.

> Problem: Everyone will bring (his? her?) own lunch.
> Solution: *Everyone* will bring *his or her* own lunch.
> Wrong: Everyone will bring *their* own lunch.

d. A pronoun is singular when its antecedent is a noun modified by *each, every, neither*, or *either*. Although these words are indefinite pronouns (29-a), they are called *indefinite adjectives* when modifying a noun. Don't mistake the indefinite adjective for the real subject.

> *Each* rabbit won *its* owner a blue ribbon.
> ₛ
>
> *Every* boy in the audience had purchased *his* own ticket.
> ₛ
>
> *Either* girl will accept *her* award with grace and modesty.
> ₛ

e. If the antecedent of a pronoun is a *collective noun* (22-d), the pronoun is singular if the group acts as a unit, plural if the members of the group act as individuals.

> Right: The jury brought in *its* verdict.
> (The members of the jury acted in unison, as one.)
>
> Right: For three hours, the jury exchanged *their* opinions.
> (The members of the jury acted individually.)

f. A pronoun referring to two antecedents connected by *and* is plural if the antecedents are different persons, animals, or things.

> (1) The captain and *the* quarterback regretted *their* shouting match on the field.
> (Repetition of the article indicates two persons.)

However, if the two antecedents refer to the same person, the pronoun is singular and the article is not repeated.

> (2) The captain and quarterback broke *his* ankle.
> (The two nouns, *captain* and *quarterback*, name the same person.)

g. A pronoun referring to two antecedents connected by *or*, *nor*, *either . . . or*, or *neither . . . nor* may be singular or plural depending on the number of the antecedents. (Note: *neither* may be followed by *nor*, but NEVER by *or*.)

> (1) Either Elsie or Jane will bring *her* Monopoly set.
> (Both *Elsie* and *Jane* are singular. Therefore, the singular pronoun *her* is correct.)

> (2) Neither the girls nor the boys kept *their* promises.
> (Both *boys* and *girls* are plural. Therefore, the plural pronoun *their* is correct.)

When one antecedent is singular and one is plural, the pronoun must agree with the nearer one.

> (3) Neither the *coach* nor his *players* have given *their* consent to the trip.
> (Since *coach* and *players* differ in number, the pronoun *their* correctly refers to the nearer antecedent, *players*.)

> (4) Neither the *players* nor the *coach* has given *his* consent.
> (Since *players* and *coach* differ in number, the pronoun *his* correctly refers to the nearer antecedent, *coach*.)

h. Sometimes the antecedent of a pronoun is not clear. Then it is necessary to rewrite the sentence or insert a noun, thus making the antecedent clear.

> (1) Unclear: The teacher told the new student that she needed three books. (Who is *she*: the teacher or the new student?)
> Clear: The teacher said that the new student needed three books.
> or: The teacher said to the new student, "You need three books."
> or: Mrs. Brown told Tim that he needed three books.

(2) Unclear: The boss distributed paychecks to his employees, but some were incorrect. (Are the paychecks or the employees incorrect?)

Clear: The boss distributed paychecks to his employees, but some of the checks were incorrect.

Unclear: He eats too fast, and this gives him a stomachache. (Here the antecedent of *this* is missing.)

Clear: Eating too fast gives him a stomachache.

37. COMMON PRONOUN ERRORS

a. A pronoun following *than* or *as* may be in the nominative or objective case, depending on the sense of the sentence.

You love my brother better than (I or me).
(There are two ways to interpret its meaning.)
You love my brother better than *I* (love him).
(*I* is correct because it is the subject of the dependent clause "than I love him.")
or: You love my brother better than (you love) *me*.
(*Me* is correct because it is the object of the dependent clause "than you love me.")

In the sentences above, either pronoun, *I* or *me*, is possible, depending on your interpretation. Sometimes there is only one possible interpretation.

My sister is taller than (I or me).
My sister is taller *than I (am tall)*.

My sister is as tall as (I or me).
My sister is as tall *as I (am tall)*.

b. Never repeat a subject by placing a personal pronoun immediately after it.

Wrong: My sister *she* is very smart.
Right: My sister is very smart.

c. A pronoun takes the same case as the noun with which it is in apposition (17).

> Wrong: *Us* girls like ice cream.
> Right: *We* girls like ice cream.
> > (*Girls* identifies *we*. Either *we* or *girls* can stand alone as the subject of the sentence. Therefore, the nominative case form *we* is required.)

> Wrong: Ice cream is enjoyed by *we* girls.
> Right: Ice cream is enjoyed by *us* girls.
> > (*Us* is in apposition with *girls*. Either *us* or *girls* can stand alone as the object of the preposition *by*. Therefore, the objective case form *us* is required.)

Easy Aid: If you need help, try the elimination trick. "(We or Us) teenagers are happy." Eliminate *teenagers*—"We are happy" or "Us are happy"? The answer is *We*. Another example: "The PTA praised (we or us) seniors." Eliminate *seniors*—"The PTA praised we" or "The PTA praised us"? The answer is *us*.

d. *Them* (objective case) should never be used as the subject of a sentence or as an adjective.

> Wrong: *Them* are my friends.
> Right: *They* are my friends.

> Wrong: I gave *them* books to Sally.
> Right: I gave *those* books to Sally.

e. Do not shift from one kind of pronoun to another within the same sentence.

> Wrong: If *someone* really wants to bowl well, *you* should practice at least twice a week.
> Right: If *you* really want to bowl well, *you* should practice at least twice a week.
> or: If *someone* really wants to bowl well, *he or she* should practice at least twice a week.

f. WHO (the nominative case) changes to WHOM in the objective case. The choice of WHO or WHOM depends on the way it is used in a phrase or clause. (See also 30–31.)

Easy Aid: If you are uncertain as to whether to use WHO or WHOM, substitute a personal pronoun (HE or HIM, SHE or HER, THEY or THEM).

(1) He is one of those drivers WHO is so polite that he honks his horn before he forces you off the road!

> (subject of the dependent clause "who is so polite")

Would you say "HE is so polite" or "HIM is so polite"? You would say HE, nominative case; therefore, you want WHO, also nominative case.

(2) Do you know WHO she is?

> (predicate pronoun completing the linking verb *is*)

Change the word order: she is _____. Remember that the nominative case follows the verb *be*: "It is *I*." "It was HE." "It was WHO."

(3) The taxi driver WHOM I flagged down said that the easiest way to kill an hour is to drive around the block!

> (object of the dependent clause "whom I flagged down")

Change the word order: I flagged _____ down. (SHE or HER?) You would choose HER; I flagged HER down. HER is objective case; therefore, you want WHOM, also objective case.

(4) Many teenagers with WHOM I have talked claim they would do less lying if their parents asked fewer questions!

> (object of the preposition *with*)

Change the word order: I have talked with _____ (THEY or THEM?) THEM, of course; therefore, you want WHOM.

VERBS

38. THE KEYWORD OF A SENTENCE: THE VERB

A **verb** is a word that expresses *action* (play, work, think) or *state of being* (is, are, become, seem). An action may be mental or physical.

(1) A little experience often *upsets* a lot of theory.

> (*Upsets* is an action verb.)

(2) The farmer *was* cross because someone *stepped* on his corn!

> (*Was* shows state of being; *stepped*—in the dependent clause—shows action.)

(3) The mosquito *bites* the hand that *feeds* it.

> (*Bites* is an action verb in the main clause; *feeds* is an action verb in the dependent clause.)

(4) A smile *is* the whisper of a laugh.

> (*Is* shows state of being.)

(5) He *thought* he had wings and could *fly*; he *was* just "plane" crazy!

> (*Thought* and *fly* are action verbs in the first main clause; *was* shows state of being in the second main clause.)

(6) Why did she *say* that fears *multiply* faster than rabbits?

> (*Say* is an action verb in the main clause; *multiply* is an action verb in the dependent clause.)

39, 40. TENSE

39. The **tense** of a verb shows the time of an action or state of being.

SIMPLE TENSES

a. The **present tense** expresses action taking place in the present.

SINGULAR	PLURAL
Person	
1st: I work	we work
2nd: you work	you work
3rd: he, she, it works	they work

I work in a factory.
He works on a farm.

Notice that the third person, singular, present tense, ends in "s."

b. The **past tense** expresses action that took place in the past.

I worked	we worked
you worked	you worked
he, she, it worked	they worked

In the past, I worked in a factory.
Yesterday he worked on a farm.

c. The **future tense** expresses action that will take place in the future.

I shall work	we shall work
you will work	you will work
he, she, it will work	they will work

I shall work in a factory next week.
Next week he will work on a farm.

Laugh Your Way Through Grammar

PERFECT TENSES

d. The **present perfect tense** expresses action in the past and continuing to the present.

I have worked   we have worked
you have worked   you have worked
he, she, it has worked   they have worked

I have worked in a factory for five years.
He has worked on a farm for five years.

e. The **past perfect tense** expresses action completed before a certain time in the past.

I had worked   we had worked
you had worked   you had worked
he, she, it had worked   they had worked

I had worked in a factory before I quit.
He had worked on a farm before his back was injured.

f. The **future perfect tense** expresses action that will be completed before a certain time in the future.

I shall have worked   we shall have worked
you will have worked   you will have worked
he, she, it will have   they will have worked
  worked

By 1998, I shall have worked in the factory for ten
  years.
By 1998, he will have worked on the farm for ten years.

40. a. Avoid unnecessary shifts in tense.

Wrong: The children *washed* the dishes in soapy water, and
        they *rinse* them carefully.
                (shift from past tense *washed* in the first
                clause to the present tense *rinse* in the
                second clause)

Right: The children *washed* the dishes in soapy water, and they *rinsed* them carefully.

Wrong: The class *congratulates* Dr. Brown when she *announced* her promotion.
            (shift from the present tense *congratulates* in the main clause to the past tense *announced* in the subordinate clause)

Right: The class *congratulated* Dr. Brown when she *announced* her promotion.

b. However, it is necessary to shift from past to present when you are stating an eternal truth.

Wrong: Columbus discovered that the world *was* round.
            (It still is round, isn't it?)

Right: Columbus discovered that the world *is* round.

41. PRINCIPAL PARTS OF VERBS

A verb has three main, or principal, parts—the *present tense*, the *past tense*, and the *past participle*. They are called the **principal parts** of a verb.

a. The past tense and the past participle of a **regular verb** are formed by adding "-d" or "-ed" to the present tense.

PRESENT TENSE	PAST TENSE	PAST PARTICIPLE
tie	tied	tied
die	died	died
talk	talked	talked

Note: The past participle, when preceded by the helping verb *have*, *has*, or *had*, is used to form the perfect tenses (39-d, e, f).

b. However, **irregular verbs** do not follow rule *a*, above. Their principal parts must be learned by memorizing them.

41-b

PRESENT	PAST	PAST PARTICIPLE
am, be	was	been
bear (carry)	bore	borne
beat	beat	beat, beaten
become	became	become
begin	began	begun
bite	bit	bitten
bleed	bled	bled
blow	blew	blown
break	broke	broken
bring	brought	brought
build	built	built
buy	bought	bought
catch	caught	caught
choose	chose	chosen
come	came	come
creep	crept	crept
cry	cried	cried
deal	dealt	dealt
dig	dug	dug
dive	dived, dove	dived
do	did	done
draw	drew	drawn
drink	drank	drunk
drive	drove	driven
dry	dried	dried
eat	ate	eaten
fall	fell	fallen
feed	fed	fed
feel	felt	felt
fight	fought	fought
find	found	found
flee	fled	fled
fly	flew	flown
forget	forgot	forgotten
forgive	forgave	forgiven
freeze	froze	frozen
fry	fried	fried
get	got	got, gotten
give	gave	given
go	went	gone

PRESENT	PAST	PAST PARTICIPLE
grow	grew	grown
hang (person)	hanged	hanged
hang (picture)	hung	hung
has, have	had	had
hear	heard	heard
hide	hid	hidden
know	knew	known
lay	laid	laid
lead	led	led
lie (recline)	lay	lain
lie (tell an un-truth)	lied	lied
lose	lost	lost
make	made	made
mean	meant	meant
meet	met	met
pay	paid	paid
ride	rode	ridden
ring	rang	rung
rise	rose	risen
run	ran	run
see	saw	seen
shake	shook	shaken
shine (polish)	shined	shined
shine (light)	shone	shone
show	showed	shown
shrink	shrank	shrunk
sing	sang	sung
sink	sank	sunk
sit	sat	sat
slay	slew	slain
sleep	slept	slept
speak	spoke	spoken
spend	spent	spent
spring	sprang	sprung
stand	stood	stood
steal	stole	stolen
sting	stung	stung
swear	swore	sworn
swim	swam	swum

PRESENT	PAST	PAST PARTICIPLE
swing	swung	swung
take	took	taken
teach	taught	taught
tear	tore	torn
tell	told	told
think	thought	thought
throw	threw	thrown
try	tried	tried
wake	woke (waked)	waked
wear	wore	worn
win	won	won
write	wrote	written

c. A few irregular verbs do not change at all, regardless of tense: burst, burst, burst; hurt, hurt, hurt; spread, spread, spread.

d. Misusing the principal parts of verbs results in serious blunders, such as: ''We seen it,'' ''He done it,'' ''I have ate.'' Below are the forms and usage of three irregular verbs. Use these as a guide for other irregular verbs.

Principal parts: see, saw, seen

Present tense: We *see* it.
Past tense: We *saw* it. (not *seen*)
Past participle: We *have seen* it.

Principal parts: do, did, done

Present tense: He *does* it.
Past tense: He *did* it. (not *done*)
Past participle: He *had done* it. (not *had did*)

Principal parts: eat, ate, eaten

Present tense: I *eat* lobster.
Past tense: I *ate* lobster.
Past participle: I *have eaten* lobster. (not *have ate*)

Note: The past participle is always preceded by the helping verb *have, has,* or *had.*

The Parts of Speech   **111**

42, 43. TRANSITIVE AND INTRANSITIVE VERBS

42. **a.** **Transitive** verbs take a direct object; **intransitive** verbs do not.

b. A **transitive verb** requires a *direct object* (7-b) to express a complete thought.

> In 1518 Cortez *brought* seventeen horses to the Western Hemi-
> *d.o.*
> sphere.
>
> George Washington *named* his favorite horse "Blue Skin."
> *d.o.*

43. **a.** An **intransitive verb** does not take a direct object.

> A carrier pigeon with its ears stuffed up cannot *fly*. (no object)
>
> Fish *cough*. (no object)

b. Some verbs are transitive in one sentence and intransitive in another.

> Max *wrote* a novel.
> *transitive d.o.*
>
> Max *wrote* rapidly. (no object)
> *intransitive*

44. LINKING VERBS

a. A **linking verb** connects the subject with a word in the predicate: a *noun*, a *pronoun*, or an *adjective*. A linking verb never takes a direct object.

> I *am* a student. (*I* and *student* refer to the same person.)
> (*Student* is a **predicate noun.**)
>
> I *am* intelligent. (*I* and *intelligent* refer to the same person.)
> (*Intelligent* is a **predicate adjective.**)

b. A pronoun that follows a linking verb is in the *nominative case* (33-d).

> The best pitcher on the team *is* she. (*Pitcher* and *she* refer to the same person. *She* is a **predicate pronoun.**)

c. The most common linking verbs are forms of the verb *be*: am, is, are, was, were, been. Others: appear, become, feel, grow, look, prove, remain, seem, smell, sound, taste, turn.

> She *became* a ballerina.
> The contestants *seem* clever.

d. Sometimes it is difficult to decide whether a verb performs in a sentence as a linking verb or as an action verb. If the verb can be replaced by some form of *be*, then it is a linking verb.

> The pecan pie *tastes* good.
>> (We can substitute a form of *be* as follows:)
> The pecan pie *is* good.
>> (This sentence makes sense; therefore, *tastes* must be a linking verb.)

> Kim *tastes* the pecan pie.
>> (Can we substitute a form of *be* for *tastes*?)
> Kim *is* the pecan pie.
>> (This sentence doesn't make sense; therefore, *tastes* must be an action verb.)

45. VOICE

The **voice** of a verb tells whether (*a*) the subject is the actor, or (*b*) the subject is acted upon. Only a transitive verb (42-a) has voice.

a. **Active voice** shows the subject is doing the action.

> The author Tobias Smollett *invented* the street-corner mail-box.
> In 1924 Simon & Schuster *published* the first book of cross-word puzzles.

b. **Passive voice** shows the subject is receiving the action.

> The street-corner mailbox *was invented* by the author Tobias Smollett.
> The first book of crossword puzzles *was published* by Simon & Schuster in 1924.

(Notice that the passive voice requires a form of the verb *be* plus the past participle. Whenever possible, when you are writing, use the active voice.)

c. Do not shift from the active voice to the passive voice within the same sentence.

> Wrong: As we wander through the forest, many small
> *active*
>
> animals and birds *are seen.*
> *passive*
>
> > (The active voice *wander* in the subordinate clause shifts to the passive voice *are seen* in the main clause.)
>
> Right: As we *wander* through the forest, we *see* many
> *active* *active*
>
> small animals and birds.

> Wrong: As Jake *chewed* on the taffy, a tooth *was broken.*
> *active* *passive*
>
> Right: As Jake *chewed* on the taffy, he *broke* a tooth.
> *active* *active*

46. MOOD

The **mood** of a verb indicates the manner of expressing an action or state of being.

a. The **indicative mood** makes a statement of fact or asks a question.

> He is going to the store.
> Is she going to the store?

b. The **imperative mood** gives a command.

Please go to the store immediately.

c. The **subjunctive mood** makes a statement that is doubtful or contrary to fact.

(1) Use *were* instead of *was* for the present tense.

Wrong: If I *was* a fish, I would point out that fishing turns men into liars.
Right: If I *were* a fish, I would point out that fishing turns men into liars.

Wrong: She acted as if she *was* still class president.
Right: She acted as if she *were* still class president.

(2) Use *had* and the past participle for the past tense.

Wrong: If I *would have known* the answer, I would have written it.
Right: If I *had known* the answer, I would have written it.

Wrong: If Noah *would have thought* of it when he entered the ark, he would have said, ''After me, the deluge!''
Right: If Noah *had thought* of it when he entered the ark, he would have said, ''After me, the deluge!''

d. Avoid unnecessary shifts in mood.

Wrong: Clean your room and then you may rest.
                imperative   *indicative*

(shift from imperative to indicative)

Right: Clean your room, and then rest.
              imperative   *imperative*

Right: After you clean your room, you may rest.
                    indicative   *indicative*

Wrong: <u>You may have ice cream</u> and <u>be quiet.</u>
indicative   *imperative*

(shift from indicative to imperative)

Right: <u>If you are quiet,</u> <u>you may have ice cream.</u>
indicative   *indicative*

47. AGREEMENT OF SUBJECT AND VERB

A verb must agree with its subject in (*a*) person and (*b*) number.

a. PERSON. A first person subject requires a verb in the first person. Similarly, a second person subject takes a verb in the second person; and a third person subject requires a verb in the third person. (See also 39-a to f.)

Wrong: I wants chocolate.
Right: I want chocolate. (first person)

Wrong: You was wrong.
Right: You were wrong. (second person)

Wrong: It don't matter.
Right: It doesn't matter. (third person)

b. NUMBER. A singular subject takes a singular verb; a plural subject takes a plural verb.

The Model-T *Ford was* seven feet high.
Blue *whales are* the biggest animals the world has ever known.

A complement (7) does not affect subject-verb agreement. For example, a singular subject requires a singular verb even if the complement is plural.

My favorite *fruit is* apples.
sing.   *pl.*

But: *Apples are* my favorite fruit.
pl.   *sing.*

c. A few nouns that are plural in form are singular in meaning. Such nouns as *news*, *politics*, *physics*, and *mathematics* take singular verbs. (See also 23-j.)

> *News is* "history shot on the wing." (Gene Fowler)
> *Politics teaches* people to use ballots instead of bullets.

Mistakes in agreement occur when the subject is compound. Should the verb be singular or plural?

d. A **compound subject** joined by *and* is plural.

> Nessie *and* Champ *are* well-known monsters.

e. If a compound subject joined by *and* names the SAME person or thing, the verb is singular. (See also 36-f.2.)

> Our math teacher and track coach *has* retired.
> (one person)

BUT: Repeat *our* before *track* if the two subject words refer to different persons or things. (See also 36-f.1.)

> Our math teacher and OUR track coach *have* retired.
> (two persons)

f. A compound subject joined by *or*; *either . . . or*; or *neither . . . nor* is singular if the two subject words are singular.

> *Nessie* or *Champ is* my favorite monster.
> Either *Nessie* or *Champ is* my favorite monster.
> Neither *Big Foot* nor *Yeti is* my favorite monster.

BUT: The verb is plural if the subject words are plural.

> *Are* either *cats* or *dogs* considered monsters?
> Neither *cats* nor *dogs are* considered monsters.

g. If the compound subject joined by *either . . . or*; or *neither . . . nor*; or by *or* or *nor* is made up of one singular word and one plural word, the number is governed by the NEARER subject word.

> Either Jack or his *brothers are* guilty.
> Either his brothers or *Jack is* guilty.

> Neither Jack nor his *sisters sing*.
> Neither his sisters nor *Jack sings*.

A prepositional phrase (65) within a sentence puzzles a writer. Which is the real subject? How does the phrase affect agreement?

h. A phrase between the subject and the verb does not ordinarily affect the agreement of subject and verb. The subject precedes the phrase; the object of the preposition at the end of the phrase is NOT the subject, as shown in the following examples.

In the jungle, one (of every four lion cubs) starves to death.
              s   *phrase*   *v*

(In this example, the verb *starves* agrees with the singular subject, *one*, NOT with the plural object of the preposition, *cubs*.

The eyelashes (of almost any elephant) are four inches long.
    s   *phrase*   *v*

(In this example, the verb *are* agrees with the plural subject, *eyelashes*, NOT with the singular object of the preposition, *elephant*.

i. If the subject is *plenty*, *abundance*, *variety*, or *rest*, the verb agrees with the object of the preposition. (This is an exception to *h* above.)

> Plenty of *people are* going. (*people* is plural)
> Plenty of *spinach is* grown here. (*spinach* is singular)

> The rest of the *boys were* rescued. (*boys* is plural)
> The rest of the *candy was* lost. (*candy* is singular)

j. If a prepositional phrase is followed by a *relative pronoun* (30), the verb of the dependent clause must agree with the antecedent of the relative pronoun. Occasionally, it is difficult to determine the antecedent; then you must look closely at the *meaning* of the sentence.

Mary is one (*of the girls*) who are helping.

(All the girls are helping, and Mary is just one of them. The antecedent of the relative pronoun *who* is *girls*, which is plural. Therefore, *are* i⸱ correct.)

BUT: Mary is *the* one (*of the girls*) who is helping.

(The article *the* changes the meaning of the sentence by indicating that Mary is the only one who is helping. The antecedent of *who* is *one*, which is singular. Therefore, *is* is correct.)

k. Ignore expressions as the following when they come between the subject and the verb: *accompanied by, as well as, including, in addition to, no less than, together with, not* . . . . Such phrases do NOT affect the agreement of subject and verb.

Mary, (together with her sisters,) *is going*.
  s

Mary and John, (as well as Mary's sister,) *are going*.
  s   v

Her *expression*, (not her words,) *is* friendly.
  s   v

Her *words*, (not her expression,) *are* friendly.
  s   v

Indefinite pronouns cause trouble. Which ones are singular, and which are plural?

l. If an *indefinite pronoun* (29) is the subject, the verb will be singular or plural depending on the number of the pronoun. Remember: most indefinite pronouns are singular (*each, one, neither, someone, everybody*), but a few are plural (*both, many, several*).

(1) *Singular indefinite pronouns:*

> *Everybody knows* that few children fear water unless soap is added.
>
> *Nobody* ever *gets* hurt on the corners of a square deal.
>
> *Is everyone* going?
>
> *Each* of his patients *is* saying that the new doctor is so mean that he keeps his stethoscope in the freezer!
>
> *Everybody* on the marriage council *insists* that snoring is "sheet music"!

(2) *Plural indefinite pronouns*:

> "*Many are* called, but *few are* chosen."
>
> *Several* of the female joggers *have* a whim to be slim!
>
> *Both* of the youngsters *think* that PTA means "Poor Tired Adults"!

Mathematical expressions can be tricky.

m. Study these examples:

> Four times two are eight.
> Four and two are six.
> Four plus two is six.
> Four minus two is two.
> Four divided by two is two.
> One-fourth of four is one.

n. If a noun indicates a measurement of space, time, or money, it is singular in meaning, even if it looks plural.

> Ten *dollars* is the price he quoted.
> Thirty *minutes* is all the time I can give you.
> Five *miles* is the distance from Tantown to Tooley.

o. If the subject is a fraction and is followed by an *of*-phrase, the verb agrees with the object of the preposition. (This is another exception to rule *h* of this section.)

One-fourth (of the *pizza*) *was* consumed.

One-fourth (of the *sandwiches*) *were* consumed.

p. The expression "*a* number of" takes a plural verb.

A number of children *are* going to the picnic.

A number of the team *are* coming with me.

BUT: "*the* number of" takes a singular verb.

The number of children going to the picnic *is* sixteen.

The number of the team who may come with me *is* limited to five.

Other problems in agreement:

q. A collective noun (22-d) takes a singular verb when the group is acting as a unit, and a plural verb when the individuals are acting independently.

(1) The *team is* playing today in Hempstead.

("team" acting as one, together)

(2) BUT: The *team are* voting today for a new captain.

("team" acting as individuals)

(3) The *class was* taught by Mr. Jones.

(4) BUT: The *class were* discussing the parts of speech.

r. (1) *It* may be an *expletive:* a word used to get a sentence started. In this case, *it* is NOT the subject.

> *It* is illegal to steal. ("to steal" is the subject. In subject-verb order: To steal is illegal.)

(2) *It* may also be an impersonal subject. In this case, *it* doesn't refer to anyone or anything specifically.

> *It* is snowing today.
> *It* is not the anchor *people* who gather the news.

>> (*It* always takes a singular verb even when followed by a plural predicate noun or pronoun, as in the above sentence.)

s. In some sentences beginning with *there is* (*are*) or *here is* (*are*), the introductory word *here* or *there* is an *expletive*, NOT the subject. The subject follows the verb.

> There *is* a monster called the Abominable Snowman in the Himalaya Mountains.

>> (In subject-verb order: A monster called the Abominable Snowman is in the Himalaya Mountains.)

> There *are* monsters called Skunk Apes living in the Florida swamp.

>> (In subject-verb order: Monsters called Skunk Apes are living in the Florida swamp.)

t. In other sentences beginning with *there is* (*are*) or *here is* (*are*), the introductory word *here* or *there* is an adverb.

> *There* (adverb) is my bus.

>> (In subject-verb order: My bus is there.)

> *Here* (adverb) are my cash and my credit card.

>> (In subject-verb order: My cash and my credit card are here.)

48–51. VERBALS

Verbals are words that begin as verbs but change both in form and in use. There are three kinds of verbals: *infinitives*, *participles*, and *gerunds*.

48. a. An **infinitive** is a verbal formed by combining *to* and a verb.

to play	to be	to smile
to joke	to have	to jump

Try to avoid splitting infinitives.

Wrong: He is going *to quickly swallow* the medicine.
Right: He is going *to swallow* the medicine quickly.

Wrong: She dared *to boldly accuse* me.
Right: She dared *to accuse* me boldly.

b. An infinitive may take a subject, an object, or a modifier.

Mother urged *us* to eat.
  (*Us* is the subject of *to eat*.)

Ms. Lopez asked the class to write a *poem*.
  (*Poem* is the object of *to write*.)

She told us to start *immediately*.
  (*Immediately* modifies *to start*.)

c. An infinitive plus one or more words forms an **infinitive phrase.** In a sentence, the phrase acts as a single unit—as a noun, an adjective, or an adverb.

d. An infinitive used as a *noun* may be a subject, object, predicate noun, or appositive.

SUBJECT:

  "*To err* is human." (infinitive)
  To milk a cow is my leading ambition. (phrase)

DIRECT OBJECT:

> They prefer *to smile*.   (infinitive)
> His mother said that she would like *to see some change in him*—so he swallowed two nickels and a dime.   (phrase)

OBJECT OF PREPOSITION:

> He asked for nothing except *to read*.   (infinitive)
> He asked for nothing except *to read the Bible and the Times*.   (phrase)

PREDICATE NOUN:

> Life is *to live*. (infinitive)
> Happiness is *to love and to be loved by the same person*. (phrase)

APPOSITIVE:

> She described her goal, *to climb*.
>> (infinitive in apposition with *goal*, the direct object)
> His wish, *to become a flight attendant*, may well come true.
>> (phrase in apposition with *wish*, the subject)

e. An infinitive used as an *adjective* modifies a noun or pronoun; when used as an *adverb*, the infinitive modifies a verb or an adjective.

ADJECTIVE:

> Give me a riddle *to solve*.
>> (infinitive modifying *riddle*, the direct object.)
> The horse *to be auctioned* had won the Derby.
>> (phrase modifying *horse*, the subject)

ADVERB:

> Are you ready *to leave*?
>> (infinitive modifying *ready*, an adjective)
> Sally dived *to save the drowning child*.
>> (phrase modifying *dived*, a verb)

f. The subject of an infinitive is in the objective case.

> The coach ordered *them* to do twenty push-ups.
> The monkey begged *Jim* and *me* to return its banana.

g. The object of an infinitive is in the objective case.

> I was asked to call *her*.
> Judd wanted to tell *me* that an acrobat turns a flop into a success.

h. The *to* of the infinitive is frequently omitted after certain verbs: dare, feel, hear, let, make, need, and see.

> A roller coaster can make your blood *(to) race* and your legs *(to) tremble*.
> I saw him *(to) go*.

49. A **participle** is a verbal used as an *adjective*.

a. The **present participle** is formed by adding *-ing* to the stem of the verb: *eating, talking, walking*. The **past participle** is formed by adding *-d* or *-ed* to the stem. The past participle is the third principal part of a verb (41): smile, smiled, *have smiled*; learn, learned, *have learned*. Some verbs are irregular: go, went, *have gone*.

b. A participle, when used alone, is a **pure adjective:** *fallen* leaves, *yelping* dog, *stored* energy.

> The *whistling* boy entered the auditorium.
> (The participle *whistling* modifies *boy*.)

c. A participle in the predicate, following a linking verb (44-a), is called a **predicate adjective.**

> The child was *frightened*.
> (The participle *frightened* modifies *child*.)

d. When used with other words, the participle forms a **participial phrase,** modifying a noun or pronoun.

> This novel, *written by Willa Cather*, was immediately popular.
>> (The participial phrase "written by Willa Cather" modifies *novel*.)

e. Punctuation Aid:

(1) A participial phrase appearing at the BEGINNING of a sentence is separated by a comma from the rest of the sentence.

> *Parked alongside a hydrant*, the car was ticketed.
> *Singing loudly*, we entered the auditorium.

(2) A participial phrase that appears in the MIDDLE of a sentence is set off by commas *if the phrase is not necessary to the meaning of the sentence*. (See 224-1.)

> The little boy, *fiddling with some marbles*, boldly challenged the class bully.
>> ("Fiddling with some marbles" is not necessary to the meaning of the sentence and therefore is set off with commas.)

(3) If the phrase is *necessary* to the meaning of the sentence, it is NOT set off with commas.

> The little boy *fiddling with marbles* is my brother.
>> ("Fiddling with marbles" identifies the little boy who is my brother and therefore is necessary and is not set off with commas.)

50. a. A **gerund** is a verbal used as a *noun*. It is formed by adding *-ing* to the stem of the verb: *dancing, chewing, walking*, etc. Don't confuse a gerund with a present participle, which also ends in *-ing*. Remember: a participle functions as an *adjective*, a gerund as a *noun*.

b. A gerund plus one or more words forms a **gerund phrase** used as a noun.

SUBJECT:

> *Blushing* is a lost art. (gerund)
> *Swallowing your pride* is good for you—and it contains no
> calories! (phrase)

DIRECT OBJECT:

> Many children love *swimming*. (gerund)
> I heard the *whispering of the wind in the trees*. (phrase)

OBJECT OF PREPOSITION:

> She dreamed of *dancing*. (gerund)
> They went to the Met for the *opening of the new opera sea-
> son*. (phrase)

PREDICATE NOUN:

> Her favorite hobby is *ice-skating*. (gerund)
> His favorite hobby is *making model airplanes*. (phrase)

APPOSITIVE:

> Her work, *teaching*, meant more to her than anything
> else. (gerund)
> She loved her work, *teaching ceramics to small chil-
> dren*. (phrase)

c. A noun or pronoun preceding a gerund usually takes the possessive
case. (35)

> We admired *Fran's handling* of the case.
> He liked *my singing*.
> His mother did not approve of *his going* away.

Be sure to draw a distinction between a gerund and a present participle, since both verbals end in *-ing*. Imagine three boys acting. Someone asks: "Which boy do you like best?" You answer:

> "I like the boy *acting* in Scene I."

The speaker likes the *boy*; *acting* is a participle identifying him.

Someone asks: "What do you like best about that boy?" You answer:

"I like the boy's acting in Scene I."

This time the speaker likes the *acting* rather than the boy; *acting* is a gerund.

d. Punctuation Aid:

A **gerund phrase** that is the subject and that appears at the beginning of a sentence is not separated by a comma from the rest of the sentence.

Studying for two hours helped me to pass the test.
(subject; no comma)

51. DANGLING VERBAL PHRASES

A **dangling modifier** occurs when a phrase has no *logical* subject to modify. The fault can be corrected by supplying a logical "doer" of the action.

(1) Wrong: Standing on a corner, two cars were seen to collide. (Obviously ridiculous: imagine two cars standing on a corner!)

Right: Standing on a corner, **we** saw two cars collide. (Now the phrase, "Standing on a corner," modifies the pronoun *we*, and the sentence makes sense.)

(2) Wrong: By studying for two hours, the test was passed. (Who studied? Who passed the test? Did the "test" do the studying?)

Right: By studying for two hours, **I** passed the test. (Now the pronoun *I* indicates who did the "studying for two hours," and the sentence makes sense.)

(3) Wrong: To play football well, running, kicking, and passing exams are necessary. (Who is playing football?)

Right: To play football well, **one** must run, kick, and pass exams! (Now the pronoun *one* indicates who might want "to play football well," and the sentence makes sense.)

ADJECTIVES

52. A MODIFIER: THE ADJECTIVE

An **adjective** is a modifier (8). As a modifier, an adjective describes or limits the meaning of a noun or pronoun.

> **descriptive adjectives:**
>
> > a *beautiful* sunset,
> > *spectacular* fireworks,
> > an *inspiring* message
>
> **limiting adjectives:**
>
> > *ten* days, *this* antique, a *few* seniors

53. WORDS THAT FUNCTION AS ADJECTIVES

Nouns, pronouns, articles, numerals, and participles—all can function as adjectives.

a. *common nouns:* a *city* street, a *family* gathering, a *diamond* ring

b. *proper nouns:* the *Canadian* capital, the *Mexican* border, the *American* flag (Note: Adjectives formed from proper nouns are called **proper adjectives.** They are always capitalized.)

c. *possessive forms of nouns and pronouns: Carla's* school, *her* graduation

d. *demonstrative pronouns: this* book, *that* song, *these* apples, *those* trees

e. *indefinite pronouns: each* girl, *every* boy, *another* reason

f. *interrogative pronouns: whose* jacket, *which* team, *what* time

g. *indefinite articles: a, an; definite article: the*

h. *numerals: five* children, the *fifth* child

i. *participles: falling* star, *cracked* egg, *broken* glass

54. POSITION OF ADJECTIVES

a. As a rule, an adjective precedes the noun it modifies.

a *good* day; the *next* chapter; a *tall, attractive* girl

b. A combination of adjectives may follow the noun.

All citizens, *rich* or *poor*, are expected to vote.
The principal, *strong, clever,* and *charming,* won the debate.

c. An adjective, called the **predicate adjective** (44-a), may be placed in the predicate of a sentence to modify the subject noun or pronoun.

Margaret was *absent* today. I am very *thirsty.*

55. DEGREES OF COMPARISON OF ADJECTIVES

Adjectives have three **degrees of comparison:** *positive, comparative,* and *superlative.*

POSITIVE	COMPARATIVE	SUPERLATIVE
big	bigger	biggest
large	larger	largest
short	shorter	shortest

a. The **positive degree** simply expresses a quality.

Jake is *tall.*   Jill is *intelligent.*

b. The **comparative degree** expresses a lower or higher degree than the positive. It draws a comparison between *two* people or objects. Most adjectives of one syllable add ''er'' to the positive. Adjectives of two or more syllables generally are formed by prefixing with ''more'' or ''less.''

One syllable: big—bigger
Two syllables: edible—more or less edible

Jake is the *taller* of the two boys.
Jill is the *more (less) intelligent* of the two girls.

c. The **superlative degree** expresses the lowest or highest degree. It draws a comparison among *three* or more people or objects. Most adjectives of one syllable add "est" to the positive. Adjectives of two or more syllables generally are formed by prefixing with "most" or "least."

> One syllable: big—biggest
> Two syllables: edible—most or least edible
>
> Jake is the *tallest* of the nine boys.
> Jill is the *most (least) intelligent* of the eight girls.

d. A few adjectives form their comparative and superlative degrees in an irregular way.

POSITIVE	COMPARATIVE	SUPERLATIVE
bad	worse	worst
far	farther, further	farthest, furthest
good	better	best
ill	worse	worst
little	less	least
many	more	most
much	more	most
several	more	most
some	more	most
well	better	best

e. If an adjective expresses an absolute quality, it should not be compared. For example: the adjective *perfect* expresses an absolute quality. There is no such thing as "more perfect" or "less perfect." Instead, use *more nearly* or *most nearly*.

> Wrong: This is the *most perfect* circle I've drawn.
> Right: This is the *most nearly perfect* circle I've drawn.

Others: *unique*; *dead*; *endless*; *square*; *straight*; *current*.

> Wrong: This is a most unique experience.
> Right: This is a *unique* experience.
>
> Wrong: The class seemed more endless than usual.
> Right: The class seemed *endless*, as usual.

f. Use "as . . . as" for positive comparisons, and "so . . . as" for negative comparisons.

> Positive: Leona is *as* pretty *as* Nell.
> Negative: Leona is not *so* pretty *as* Nell.

56. COMMON ADJECTIVE ERRORS

a. Most one- and two-syllable adjectives ending in *y* form their comparative and superlative degrees in the regular manner: add -er and -est to the positive. First, though, change *y* to *i*, as below.

POSITIVE	COMPARATIVE	SUPERLATIVE
happy	happier	happiest
pretty	prettier	prettiest
dry	drier	driest
lovely	lovelier	loveliest
silly	sillier	silliest
noisy	noisier	noisiest
easy	easier	easiest

b. When the comparative degree of an adjective is used with *than*, the words *other* or *else* must be used also.

> Wrong: He is taller than any boy in his class.
> Right: He is taller than any *other* boy in his class.

Use common sense on this one: He cannot be taller than any boy in his class, since *he* is in his class. But he can be taller than any *other* boy in his class.

> Wrong: That man is richer than any man in America.
> Right: That man is richer than any *other* man in America.

(But it is correct to write: "That woman is richer than any man in America.")

c. Avoid the **double comparison** error. Use either the ''-er'' or ''more'' method to form the comparative degree (55-b), but do not use both methods together. The same rule applies when forming the superlative degree (55-c).

>Wrong: Jake is the *more taller* of the two boys.
>Right: Jake is the *taller* of the two boys.

>Wrong: Jake is the *most tallest* of the nine boys.
>Right: Jake is the *tallest* of the nine boys.

d. When an adjective and a noun are combined to form a compound adjective, use the singular form of the noun.

>The teacher gave her students a forty-*minute* recess.
>They built a six-*foot* wall around their home.

BUT . . .

>The recess was forty *minutes* long.
>The wall is six *feet* high.

Easy Aid: If the modifier comes BEFORE the noun, it should be singular. If the modifier comes AFTER the noun, it should be plural.

e. Some nouns keep their SINGULAR form when preceded by an adjective expressing a number. (Examples: *dozen, gross, score, head, hundred, million, thousand.*)

>I would like *three dozen* eggs. (not three dozens)
>There are *two million* stars in the sky. (not two millions)
>The manager ordered *six gross* of pencils. (not six grosses)

When the number is not specified, the PLURAL form should be used.

>*Dozens* of eggs flooded the market.
>There are *millions* of stars in the sky.
>*Grosses* of pencils are still in the storehouse.

f.   When two or more adjectives or nouns refer to the SAME person or thing, use an article (*a*, *an*, *the*) before the first adjective or noun only.

> We purchased *the* white and green house.
>
> > (one house)
>
> *The* red, white, and blue flag is ours.
>
> > (one flag)
>
> John is *a* waiter and busboy.
>
> > (one person doing two jobs)

When two or more adjectives or nouns refer to DIFFERENT persons or things, use an article before *each* adjective or noun.

> We purchased *the* white and *the* green houses.
>
> > (two houses)
>
> *A* red, *a* white, and *a* blue flag flew over the stadium.
>
> > (three flags)
>
> *A* waiter and *a* busboy hovered over our table.
>
> > (two persons)

g.   Use *a* before a noun beginning with a consonant. Use *an* before a noun beginning with a vowel.

> He bought a giraffe, an elephant, and a hound.
> An apple, an orange, and a pear are in the refrigerator.

h.   Use the "-ed" ending for compound adjectives that describe an animate creature: a right-hand*ed* pitcher or a four-legg*ed* animal. Do *not* use the "-ed" ending for compound adjectives that describe an inanimate object: average-size car or long-sleeve shirt.

Laugh Your Way Through Grammar

ADVERBS

57, 58. ANOTHER MODIFIER: THE ADVERB

An **adverb** describes or limits the meaning of a verb, an adjective, or another adverb. Like the adjective, an adverb is a modifier (8).

57. An adverb modifies a verb.

An adverb may be placed before a verb, after a verb, or within a verb phrase.

> *Usually* the game of love *ends* in a tie.
> adv.   v

> Ideas die *quickly* in some heads because they can't stand sol-
>   v   adv.
>
> itary confinement!

> Ida has *frequently* performed for our troops.
> adv.
> — verb phrase —

58. An adverb may modify an adjective or another adverb.

MODIFYING AN ADJECTIVE:

> She is *exceedingly* intelligent.
> adv.   adj.

> The *rather* futile effort failed.
> adv.   adj.

MODIFYING AN ADVERB:

He writes *very cleverly*.
adv.　　adv.

Don't row *too far* from shore.
adv. adv.

59. ADVERBS EXPRESS TIME, PLACE, DEGREE, MANNER

a. Adverbs may be classified according to meaning.

TIME adverbs answer the question WHEN.
yesterday, today, now, later

PLACE adverbs answer the question WHERE.
here, there, inside, nowhere

DEGREE adverbs answer the question TO WHAT EXTENT.
more, less, rather, very

MANNER adverbs answer the question HOW.
politely, stubbornly, happily, surely

b. A noun may be used as an adverb of TIME or PLACE.

We will leave *Monday* for Washington.
n.

(*Monday*, a noun used as an adverb, modifies the verb *will leave*.)

When will you come *home*?
n.

(*Home*, a noun used as an adverb, modifies the verb *will come*.)

60. FORMING ADVERBS FROM ADJECTIVES

a. Many adverbs are formed by adding *-ly* to adjectives.

ADJECTIVE	ADVERB
usual	usually
beautiful	beautifully
scarce	scarcely
happy	happily
angry	angrily

b. Spelling Aids:

(1) The regular rule: add *-ly* directly to the adjective.

scarce—scarcely

(2) When adding *-ly* to an adjective ending in *l*, be sure to keep the *-l* ending of the adjective.

usual—usually

(3) When adding *-ly* to an adjective ending in *-y*, change the *-y* to *i*.

angry—angrily

61. INTERROGATIVE ADVERBS

An **interrogative adverb** begins a question.

Where are they going?
They are going *where*? (subject-verb order)

(*Where* modifies the verb *are going*.)

How are you going to ice the cake?
Why did you do it?
When will he graduate?

62. DEGREES OF COMPARISON OF ADVERBS

Adverbs, like adjectives, have **degrees of comparison:** *positive, comparative*, and *superlative*. The rules for comparing adverbs are the same as those for comparing adjectives (55).

a. The **positive degree** simply states a quality.

> Jane drove *fast*.
> Dick drove *carefully*.

b. The **comparative degree** expresses a lower or higher degree than the positive. It draws a comparison between *two* people or objects. Most adverbs of one syllable add ''er'' to the positive. Adverbs of two or more syllables generally are formed by prefixing with ''more'' or ''less.''

> One syllable: fast—faster
> Two syllables: quickly—more or less quickly
>
> Jane drove *faster* than Dick.
> Dick drove *more (less) carefully* than Jane.

c. The **superlative degree** expresses the lowest or highest degree. It draws a comparison among *three* or more people or objects. Most adverbs of one syllable add ''est'' to the positive. Adverbs of two or more syllables generally are formed by prefixing with ''most'' or ''least.''

> One syllable: fast—fastest
> Two syllables: quickly—most or least quickly.
>
> Of the four contestants, Jane drove the *fastest*.
> Of the three contestants, Dick drove the *most (least) carefully*.

d. A few adverbs form their comparative and superlative degrees in an irregular way.

POSITIVE	COMPARATIVE	SUPERLATIVE
badly	worse	worst
far	farther, further	farthest, furthest
little	less	least
much	more	most
well	better	best

63. COMMON ADVERB ERRORS

a. Be sure to use the correct form of the following adverbs:

WRONG	RIGHT
anywheres	anywhere
somewheres	somewhere
nowheres	nowhere
firstly	first

b. Don't use a negative to split an infinitive.

Wrong: I chose *to* not *go* to class.
Right: I chose not *to go* to class.

c. *No* and *not* (*n't*) are, of course, negatives. So are "never, hardly, scarcely, neither, nobody, nothing, none." Avoid the **double negative.**

Wrong: I am not in no shape to exercise.
Right: I am not in *any* shape to exercise.
Right: I am in no shape to exercise.

Wrong: Nobody never tells me what's going on.
Right: Nobody *ever* tells me what's going on.

Wrong: I hardly never get a chance to answer.
Right: I hardly *ever* get a chance to answer.

Wrong: They have*n't* done *nothing*.
Right: They have*n't* done *anything*.
Right: They have done *nothing*.

d. Do not use an adjective for an adverb.

Wrong: He is *sure* clever.
            adj.

Right: He is *surely* clever.
            adv.

Easy Aid: Substitute the adverb *very* for the problem modifier.

Wrong: The movie is *real* scary.   (VERY scary? Yes.)
            adj.

Right: The movie is *really* scary.
            adv.

Very works, so the adverb *really* is correct.

e. Don't use an adverb instead of an adjective after a **linking verb** (44-c).

Wrong: This egg smells *badly*.
            adv.

Right: This egg smells *bad*.
            adj.

Wrong: The roast tastes *well*.
            adv.

Right: The roast tastes *good*.
            adj.

f. Certain adjectives may be used instead of adverbs in *idiomatic* expressions: expressions that are acceptable because they have been used for a long time. For example, you might say to someone: "Come close." You would never say: "Come closely." Another familiar idiom is found in this expression: "Deer crossing. Drive slow."

g. Be sure that adverbs such as *only* and *just* are placed correctly. A change in placement can change the meaning of the sentence.

> *Only she* participated in two committees.
>
>> (no one else did—only *she*)

> She *only participated* in two committees.
>
>> (she participated; she didn't chair or take a leading role)

> She participated in *only two* committees.
>
>> (not in three or four)

h. Avoid the **double comparison** error. To form the comparative degree of an adverb, use either the ''-er'' or ''more'' method (62-b), but do not use both methods together. The same rule applies when forming the superlative degree (62-c). This ''double comparison'' principle is the same as 56-c.

> Wrong: Jane drove *more faster* than Dick.
> Right: Jane drove *faster* than Dick.

> Wrong: Of the four contestants, Jane drove the *most fastest*.
> Right: Of the four contestants, Jane drove the *fastest*.

PREPOSITIONS

64. A JOINING WORD: THE PREPOSITION

a. A **preposition** is a word that shows the relationship between a noun or a pronoun and some other word in the sentence.

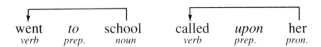

went   *to*   school   called   *upon*   her
verb   *prep.*   *noun*   *verb*   *prep.*   *pron.*

b. The noun or pronoun that follows a preposition is called the **object of the preposition.**

for a *dollar*   after *us*
    obj.   *obj.*

on the *plane*   between *them* and *us*
     obj.   *(compound object)*

65. PREPOSITIONAL PHRASES

A **prepositional phrase** includes the preposition, the object of the preposition, and modifiers of the object.

At the next corner, turn right.
     phrase

at = preposition
corner = object of the preposition
the and *next* modify *corner*

The baby crawled under the breakfast table.
                 phrase

under = preposition
table = object of the preposition
the and *breakfast* modify *table*

66. FREQUENTLY USED PREPOSITIONS

a. A **simple preposition** is a one-word preposition. Here are the most often used prepositions.

aboard	behind	in	throughout
about	below	inside	to
above	beneath	into	toward
across	beside	of	under
after	between	off	underneath
against	beyond	on	until
along	by	out	unto
among	down	outside	up
around	during	over	upon
as	except	pending	with
at	for	since	within
before	from	through	without

b. A **phrasal preposition** is a preposition made up of two or more words.

according to my favorite weather forecaster
because of my preference for tigers
due to her star-studded past
from across the wild and stormy seas
from among the seven stalwart brothers
from between the two towering silver birches
from under the gaily-decorated dock
in accordance with your clear but unpleasant instructions
in front of the madly jeering crowd
in place of her original two-hour speech
in spite of his deep, unreasoning antagonism
on account of the Abominable Snowman
out of this century's most bitter election
with regard to your recent absurd proposal

67. THE PART OF SPEECH OF A WORD DEPENDS ON ITS USE IN A SENTENCE

Words that are ordinarily prepositions may sometimes be used as adverbs or conjunctions.

preposition: We talked *before* dinner.

> *Before* shows the relationship between *dinner*, its object, and *talked*.

adverb: We talked about this *before*.

> *Before* has no object in this sentence.
> *Before* modifies *talked*, a verb.
> *Before* is therefore a TIME adverb (59) answering the question "when."

conjunction: We talked *before* we had dinner.

> *We talked* = an independent clause.
> *Before we had dinner* = a dependent clause.
> *Before*, a subordinate conjunction (72), connects the two clauses.

68. ADJECTIVE AND ADVERB PHRASES

a. Prepositional phrases are modifiers (8). A phrase that modifies a noun or a pronoun is called an **adjective phrase.**

> A book *in the hand* is worth two *in the library*.
> ("In the hand" modifies *book*; "in the library" modifies *two*.)

> *With his carrot-red hair*, he knew he would be easily recognized.
> (The phrase modifies the pronoun *he*.)

> Swimming *at the beach* is my favorite pastime.
> (The phrase modifies the gerund [verbal noun] *swimming*.)

b. A phrase that modifies a verb, an adjective, or an adverb is an **adverb phrase.**

> The dictionary is the only place where success comes *before work.*
>
>> (The phrase modifies the verb *comes.*)
>
> Jacqueline, whistling *in the dark,* showed a special kind of courage.
>
>> (The phrase modifies the participle [verbal adjective] *whistling.*)
>
> Later *in the day* we visited the new mall.
>
>> (The phrase modifies the adverb *Later.*)

69. COMMON PREPOSITION ERRORS

a. Often a preposition is incorrectly tacked on to a word. Watch the following.

WRONG	RIGHT
all of the girls	all the girls
blame on me	blame me
continue on with the work	continue with the work
cover over the desk	cover the desk
off of the table	off the table
out of the window	out the window
plan on a party	plan a party
remember of a song	remember a song
where at he went	where he went
where to he went	where he went

b. *Without* is a preposition. Never use it in place of *unless* or *that*.

> Wrong: I never go to the circus without I think of my first visit.
>
> Right: I never go to the circus that I do not think of my first visit.
>
> or: I never go to the circus without thinking of my first visit.

> Wrong: Jake won't play without he can use his favorite bat.
>
> Right: Jake won't play unless he can use his favorite bat.
>
> or: Jake won't play without his favorite bat.

c. The object of a preposition may be a dependent clause (6-b). Confusion arises when the clause is introduced by *who* or any of its forms.

> Right: We have no information about *who caused the accident*.
>
> > (*Who* is not the object of the preposition *about* but the subject of its own clause; therefore, the nominative case is correct.)

> Right: Go camping with *whomever you wish*.
>
> > (*Whomever* is not the object of the preposition *with* but the object of its own clause.)

CONJUNCTIONS

70. A CONNECTING WORD: THE CONJUNCTION

A **conjunction** is a word that connects words, phrases, or clauses. Conjunctions are classified as *coordinate* and *subordinate*. A coordinate conjunction connects sentence parts of equal importance, while a subordinate conjunction connects a less important part to a more important one.

71. COORDINATE CONJUNCTIONS

A **coordinate conjunction** connects (*a*) words, (*b*) phrases, or (*c*) clauses of equal structural rank. **And, but,** and **or** are coordinate conjunctions.

a. WORDS:

> *Mary* **and** *Martin* washed the dishes.
>> (The coordinate conjunction *and* connects two nouns.)

> Mary *washed* **and** *dried* the dishes.
>> (The coordinate conjunction *and* connects two verbs.)

b. PHRASES:

> I will meet you *at the bus stop* **or** *in Joe's restaurant.*
>> (The coordinate conjunction *or* connects two prepositional phrases.)

> I was asked *to write a quatrain* **and** *to read it in class.*
>> (The coordinate conjunction *and* connects two infinitive phrases.)

c. CLAUSES:

> *Luis trimmed the hedges,* **but** *he refused to mow the lawn.*
>> (The coordinate conjunction *but* connects two independent clauses (6-a).

The President does not desire another term of office, **nor** *would he accept a nomination.*

> (The coordinate conjunction *nor* connects two independent clauses.)

Note: These two sentences are examples of the compound sentence (11-b).

72. SUBORDINATE CONJUNCTIONS

a. A **subordinate conjunction** connects a dependent clause with an independent clause. (See 6, clauses.)

> Dinner will not be served until you are here.
>
>   *independent clause*   *dependent clause*

> (*Until* is a subordinate conjunction that connects the dependent clause with the independent clause.)

> Because the field was muddy, the game was canceled.
>
>   *dependent clause*   *independent clause*

> (*Because* is a subordinate conjunction connecting the dependent clause with the independent clause.)

Note: These two sentences are examples of the complex sentence (11-c).

b. Study these frequently used subordinate conjunctions. The relative pronouns (30), are starred.

after	if	when
although	since	where
as	*that	wherever
as if	though	*which
because	unless	while
before	until	*who
except	*what	why

73. CORRELATIVE CONJUNCTIONS

Correlative conjunctions are used in pairs.

as much . . . as	not . . . but
both . . . and	not merely . . . but
either . . . or	not only . . . but
first . . . second	not only . . . but also
less . . . than	not so much . . . as
more . . . than	now . . . then
neither . . . nor	whether . . . or

Either Martha *or* Louise will do the shopping.

Dick is *not only* our team captain *but also* our star quarterback.

Do you know *whether* Betty skates *or* skiis?

74. CONJUNCTIVE ADVERBS

Conjunctive adverbs are part conjunction and part adverb. A conjunctive adverb separates two independent clauses with the help of a semicolon. The following are conjunctive adverbs.

consequently	moreover
furthermore	nevertheless
hence	on the other hand
however	therefore

The film was boring; *consequently*, we left early.

Many homes were destroyed by the tornado; *however*, the Red Cross came to the aid of the homeless villagers.

Note: The above two sentences are examples of the compound sentence (11-b).

Punctuation Aid:

Notice that—most of the time—a comma is used after the conjunctive adverb.

> I studied day and night; therefore, I earned a high score on the SAT test.

> He is not, however, a promising candidate.

> She is a brilliant speaker; furthermore, she has an exciting and challenging program.

75. COMMON CONJUNCTION ERRORS

a. Use *and*, *but*, and *or* to connect expressions similar in structure. (See also parallel structure, 20).

> Wrong: She likes *to hike* and *swimming*. (connecting an infinitive and a gerund)
>
> Right: She likes *to hike* and *to swim*. (connecting two infinitives)
>
> Right: She likes *hiking* and *swimming*. (connecting two gerunds)

> Wrong: He enjoys *visiting* the various countries of Europe in the spring and *to study* their cultures. (connecting a gerund and an infinitive)
>
> Right: He enjoys *visiting* the various countries of Europe in the spring and *studying* their cultures. (connecting two gerunds)

b. When a subordinate conjunction introduces two or more clauses of equal importance, the conjunction should be repeated before each clause.

> Wrong: She announced *that* she was going to France and her sister would take over the business.
>
> Right: She announced *that* she was going to France and *that* her sister would take over the business.

c. Use the conjunction *than* (not *then*) after a comparative expression.

>Right: She was brighter *than* I thought.
>Right: Max was taller *than* Ellie.

d. If *say*, *think*, or *feel* is followed by an infinitive, use *that* before the infinitive.

>Wrong: Jacqueline thought to go back to school would be difficult.
>Right: Jacqueline thought *that* to go back to school would be difficult.

>Wrong: Philip said to go by boat would be more fun.
>Right: Philip said *that* to go by boat would be more fun.

e. Use *as . . . as* to express positive comparison.

>Wrong: Jill is clever *as* Marsha.
>Right: Jill is *as* clever *as* Marsha.

f. *Where* is a conjunction indicating place or position.

>Right: He is going to Chicago where he will take up residence.

Do not use *where* in place of *that*.

>Wrong: I read in an old almanac *where* mittens are merely gloves that are all thumbs!
>Right: I read in an old almanac *that* mittens are merely gloves that are all thumbs!

g. Use *so* to mean "with the result that."

>Right: She had studied hard, *so* she passed the test.

Use *so that* to express purpose.

> Wrong: She studied *so* she would pass the test.
> Right: She studied *so that* she would pass the test.

h. Do not confuse *when* and *than*. *When* follows "scarcely" and "hardly."

> Wrong: She had hardly been seated *than* the main speaker began.
> Right: She had hardly been seated *when* the main speaker began.

INTERJECTIONS

76. AN EXPLOSION OF THE MIND: THE INTERJECTION

An **interjection** is a word thrown into a sentence to show surprise or strong feeling. Some common interjections are *oh! ah! ouch! wow!*

> *Oh*! The tire is flat.
> *Ouch*! That hurts.

Any other part of speech—noun, adjective, adverb, etc.—may be used as an interjection.

> *Good*! I like that.
> "*Fire!*" she shouted.

Punctuation: An *exclamation point* (229) is placed at the end of an interjection, followed by a capital letter—if the interjection shows *strong* feeling. However, if the exclamation is *mild*, a comma is used at the end of the interjection, followed by a small letter.

> *No*! He did not reveal your secret.
> *Well*, look who's here.

SECTION IV

Problem Words and Expressions

Continued on Following Page

153

77. ACCEPT—EXCEPT

. . . **accept:**   verb meaning "to take," "to agree to"

I *accept* your payment.

. . . **except:**   preposition meaning "but," "not including"

Everyone went *except* Jim.

78. ACCOMPANIED BY—ACCOMPANIED WITH

. . . **accompanied by:**   Use with a person.

Gina was *accompanied by* Max.

. . . **accompanied with:**   Use with a thing.

The hurricane winds were *accompanied with* hail.

79. ADAPT—ADOPT

. . . **adapt:**   to adjust to a new situation; to change

You must try to *adapt* to country living.

. . . **adopt:**   to choose and accept without change

If you *adopt* our customs, you will soon find yourself at ease.

80. ADVICE—ADVISE

. . . **advice:**   noun meaning "opinion given as to how to handle a situation"

The UN gave this *advice*: handle China with care and don't devour Turkey.

. . . **advise:**   verb meaning "to give advice to"

The UN will *advise* its members to handle China with care and not to devour Turkey.

81. AFFECT—EFFECT

. . . **affect:**   verb meaning "to alter," "to change"
This new law *affects* my tax payment.

. . . **effect:**   noun meaning "result"
The *effect* of the law is that my taxes will rise.

. . . **effect:**   verb meaning "to bring about"
This new law will *effect* a tax change.

82. AGGRAVATE—IRRITATE

. . . **aggravate:**   verb meaning "to make worse"; usually used with things
Your antagonism is only *aggravating* the problem.

. . . **irritate:**   verb meaning "to provoke," "to annoy"; often used with people
Your constant tardiness *irritates* your parents.

83. AGREE TO—AGREE WITH

. . . **agree to:**   Use with a thing.
We *agree to* the plan to list rattlesnake on the menu as "prairie eel."

. . . **agree with:**   Use with a person.
Justin *agrees with* the food critic who claims that canned rattlesnake and rattlesnake soup are becoming popular in the U.S.

84. AIN'T

. . . Always incorrect; use "isn't" or "aren't."
Wrong: It *ain't* so.
Right: It *isn't* so.

Wrong: They *ain't* here.
Right: They *aren't* here.

85. ALL—ALL OF

. . . Use **all of** only with pronouns.

> *All of us* are going.
> *All of them* passed the test.

. . . Use **all** with nouns.

> *All the girls* are going.
> *All the students* passed the test.

86. ALL TOGETHER—ALTOGETHER

. . . **all together:** all at one time, usually used in a physical sense

> We were *all together* at the optician's office when we saw the sign: EYES EXAMINED WHILE YOU WAIT!

. . . **altogether:** entirely, completely

> Lena was *altogether* happy.

87. ALLUSION—ILLUSION

. . . **allusion:** indirect reference to

> Millie made an *allusion* to the Greek god Zeus.

. . . **illusion:** a hallucination; a false perception

> That the trees appeared blue was only an *illusion* caused by the mingling of light and shadow.

88. ALMOST—MOST

. . . **almost:** an adverb meaning "nearly"

> *Almost* all winter sports are characterized by settings of ice, snow, and bones!

. . . **most:** a pronoun or an adjective meaning "more than half"

> *Most* winter sports are characterized by settings of ice, snow, and bones!

Problem Words and Expressions 157

89. ALOT—A LOT—LOTS

. . . **alot:**   always wrong

Wrong: *Alot* of people think Easter Sunday is Decoration Day!

Right: Many people think Easter Sunday is Decoration Day!

. . . **A lot** and **lots** are correct for "parcels of land." As slang, these terms are acceptable in speech but not in writing.

Wrong: She bought *a lot* of candy.

Right: She bought a *good deal* of candy.

or: She bought *much* candy.

90. ALREADY—ALL READY

. . . **already:**   adverb expressing by or before a certain time

The train had *already* left.

If you can substitute "by now," *already* is correct.

The train had (by now) left.

. . . **all ready:**   adjective phrase expressing complete readiness

We were *all ready* for the trip.

If you can substitute "completely" for "all," *all ready* is correct.

We were (completely) ready for the trip.

91. ALRIGHT—ALL RIGHT

. . . **alright:**   never correct

. . . **all right:**   meaning "everything correct"

The proposed plan was *all right.*

92. AMONG—BETWEEN

. . . **among:**   Use when discussing three or more persons or things.

> Mom divided the pie *among* Alex, Matt, and me.

. . . **between:**   Use when discussing two persons or things.

> Mom divided the pie *between* Alex and me.

93. AMOUNT—NUMBER

. . . **amount:**   for bulk items that cannot be counted: spinach, money, anger, friendship, squash

> He asked for a small *amount* of maple syrup.

. . . **number:**   for individual items that can be counted: dollars, eggs, potatoes, friends, walnuts

> He learned that a large *number* of "syrup" trees are 200 to 300 years old.

94. ANGEL—ANGLE

. . . **angel:**   a heavenly creature; someone as good as an angel

> Kim said the two children were absolute *angels*, and she would be happy to take care of them at another time.

. . . **angle:**   a figure made by two lines extending from the same point; a point of view

> His *angle* in his speech is that children should be heard as well as seen.

95. ANGRY—MAD

. . . **angry:**   strongly annoyed

> The teacher was *angry* with Jeff.

. . . **mad:**   crazy; insane

> The *mad* dog bayed at the moon.

96. ANGRY AT—ANGRY WITH—ANGRY ABOUT

. . . **angry at:**   Use with an animal.

Sheila was *angry at* the hamster.

. . . **angry with:**   Use with a person.

Max was *angry with* his sister.

. . . **angry about:**   Use with a situation.

Max was *angry about* the situation in Asia.

97. ANXIOUS—EAGER

. . . **anxious:**   to be worried about something

Jill was *anxious* about the expedition on Mt. Everest.

. . . **eager:**   to look forward to; having a keen desire

Jill was *eager* to join the expedition.

98. ANYONE—ANY ONE

. . . **anyone:**   indefinite pronoun meaning ''any person; anybody''

Never argue with *anyone*: the other fellow has a right to his own idiotic ideas!

. . . **any one:**   adjective–pronoun combination meaning ''any single person or single thing''

Any one of the members is eligible.
Any one of the plans is acceptable.

99. ARRIVE IN—ARRIVE AT

. . . **arrive in:**   Use with a city or town.

Darryl *arrived in* New Orleans on Tuesday morning.

. . . **arrive at:**   Use with a small area.

Darryl *arrived at* the ballfield on Tuesday morning.

100. ASCENT—ASSENT

. . . **ascent:** the act of rising; an upward slope

The *ascent* of Mt. Everest is a challenge.

. . . **assent:** to agree to

Jack gave his *assent* to Syl's proposal.

101. AT (as an unnecessary word)

. . . Do not use unnecessarily with "where."

Wrong: *Where* is the pen *at?*

Right: *Where* is the pen?

102. AWHILE—A WHILE

. . . **awhile:** adverb

Stay *awhile*.

. . . **a while:** article plus noun; use as object of the preposition "for"

Rest *for a while* before you go out.

103. BAD—BADLY

. . . **bad:** predicate adjective meaning "ill"

I felt *bad*. (meaning "I felt ill.")

(See *feel* as a linking verb, 44-a, c.)

. . . **bad:** predicate adjective used to express sorrow or regret

I felt *bad* when they agreed that the future isn't what it used to be.

. . . **badly:** adverb meaning "very much"

The driveway is *badly* in need of repairs.
She wanted *badly* to win first prize.

104. BECAUSE OF—DUE TO

. . . because of: adverb phrase modifying a verb, adjective, or another adverb

Wrong: She was absent due to illness.

Right: She was absent *because of* illness.
(modifies the adjective "absent")

Wrong: He yelled due to the pain.

Right: He yelled *because of* the pain.
(modifies the verb "yelled")

. . . due to: adjective phrase modifying a noun or acting as a predicate adjective

Wrong: Her absence, because of illness, was recorded.

Right: Her absence, *due to* illness, was recorded.
(modifies the noun "absence")

Wrong: Her absence was because of illness.

Right: Her absence was *due to* illness.
(refers to the noun "absence")

105. BEING THAT or BEING AS—change to BECAUSE or SINCE

. . . Being that and **being as** are colloquial and should not be used in writing.

Wrong: *Being that* they live in clocks, cuckoos never have nests!

Right: *Since* they live in clocks, cuckoos never have nests!

Wrong: *Being as* you are unhappy, I'll forgive you.

Right: *Because* you are unhappy, I'll forgive you.

106. BESIDE—BESIDES

. . . **beside:** preposition meaning "by the side of"

Work *beside* me.

. . . **besides:** preposition meaning "in addition to"

Besides Koko, only Anne stood by me during the trial.

107. BORN—BORNE

. . . **born:** past tense of **bear**, meaning "bring forth by birth"

Abel was *born* at 1 a.m. on July 4th.

. . . **borne:** present perfect tense of **bear**, meaning "carry"

Charles has *borne* his brother's dishonesty for thirty years.

108. BREATH—BREATHE

. . . **breath:** a noun meaning a "portion of air"

Maria took a deep *breath* before diving.

. . . **breathe:** a verb meaning "to inhale some air"

Under water, a human being cannot *breathe* without help.

109. BRING—TAKE

. . . **bring:** indicates movement *toward* the speaker

Ms. John said, "Please *bring* your test papers to me."

. . . **take:** indicates movement *away from* the speaker

Ms. John said, "Please *take* this note to the office."

110. CAN—MAY

. . . **can:** suggests ability
I *can* jog for five miles without stopping. (I have the ability to . . .)

. . . **may:** suggests permission
Mother says I *may* jog after I have finished the dishes. (I have permission to . . .)

111. CANNOT

. . . **cannot:** Always spelled as one word.
Wrong: Insects *can not* close their eyes.
Right: Insects *cannot* close their eyes.

Exception: When "can" is followed by "not only," "can" and "not" are *not* linked.
Right: A bee can not only flap its wings 18,000 times in one minute but can also carry more than 300 times its own weight.

112. CANVAS—CANVASS

. . . **canvas:** (noun) a type of closely woven fabric
The tent was made of *canvas*.

. . . **canvass:** (verb) to ask for orders or political support
Lou *canvassed* the neighborhood to acquire additional support for his candidate.

113. CAPITAL—CAPITOL

. . . **capital:** main; wealth; seat of government
(1) The *capital* reason for his success is his willingness to work hard.
(2) He invested his *capital* in the bank so that it would earn interest.
(3) The letter "E" is like London because it is the *capital* in England!

. . . **Capitol:** (capitalized) the building in which Congress meets
The difference between America's *Capitol* and America's *capital* is that the first is in Washington and the second is in the stock market!

114. CITE—SIGHT—SITE

. . . **cite:** to quote; to state (Must be followed by a noun.)

Wilson *cited*, as proof, Arthur's confession.

. . . **sight:** to see (verb) or something seen (noun)

Bart *sighted* the comet at 3 a.m.

The most poignant *sight* in Washington, D.C., is the Vietnam Memorial.

. . . **site:** location

We chose that *site* because of the many silver birches.

115. COMPARE TO—COMPARE WITH

. . . **compare to:** used to point out similarities between two quite different things

Inflation can be *compared to* an automobile without brakes.

Compare Jenny *to* a peach, and you will see what I mean about her having a lovely complexion.

. . . **compare with:** used to point out similarities and differences between two objects or persons

This house *compares* favorably *with* our old one.

Compare Jenny *with* Jeanie, and you will see why I thought they were sisters.

116. COMPLEMENT—COMPLIMENT

. . . **complement:** that which completes

This red scarf is the perfect *complement* for a basically black outfit.

. . . **compliment:** praise

Compliments are like perfume—meant to be inhaled, not swallowed!

117. CONCUR WITH—CONCUR IN—CONCUR TO

. . . concur with: Use with persons. (''concur''—to act together to a common end; to agree)

He *concurred with* the rest of the committee about the best solution.

. . . concur in: Use to suggest joint action.

She *concurred in* the plan to eliminate littering.

. . . concur to: Use ''concur'' with an infinitive.

He *concurred to* prevent the opposition party from being successful.

118. CONTINUAL—CONTINUOUS

. . . continual: repeated, but with interruptions

Jane's *continual* questions bothered me.

. . . continuous: constant, with no interruptions

The fire alarm bell rang *continuously* for five minutes.

119. COULD OF—MAY OF—MIGHT OF—MUST OF—SHOULD OF—WOULD OF

. . . could of: Always incorrect; use ''could have.''

You *could have* told me that a porcupine has 30,000 quills.

They *must have* known that a flying fox is really a bat that glides.

''Of'' is a preposition and cannot be used as a helping (auxiliary) verb. ''Have'' is the correct auxiliary to form the verb phrases above.

120. COUNCIL—COUNSEL

. . . **council:**   (noun) a committee; a local governing body

We went to the Student *Council* for help.

. . . **counsel:**   (noun) advice

We went to the Student Council for *counsel*.

. . . **counsel:**   (verb) to give advice

He *counseled* them to avoid reckless behavior.

121. DESERT—DESSERT

. . . **desert:**   (accent on first syllable) noun meaning ''arid land''

The camel is sometimes called the ship of the *desert*.

. . . **desert:**   (accent on second syllable) verb meaning ''to abandon''

Rats *desert* a sinking ship.

. . . **dessert:**   (accent on second syllable) noun meaning ''a sweet course served at the end of a meal''

We had ice cream for *dessert*.

122. DIE OF—DIE FROM—DIE BY

. . . **die of:**   He *died of* tuberculosis.

. . . **die from:**   He *died from* exposure.

. . . **die by:**   He *died by* violence.

123. DIFFER FROM—DIFFERENT FROM—DIFFERENTLY FROM

. . . Use **from** after **differ**, **different**, or **differently**—not ''than.''

Wrong: His homework is *different than* mine.
Right: His homework is *different from* mine.

Wrong: His homework *differs than* mine.
Right: His homework *differs from* mine.

124. DIFFER FROM—DIFFER WITH

... **differ from:** Use to indicate a difference between persons or things.

My freezer *differs from* yours in that mine is larger and is self-defrosting.

... **differ with:** Use to indicate a difference of opinion.

He *differed with* me about who should receive the award.

125. DISINTERESTED—UNINTERESTED

... **disinterested:** impartial, not biased

Jack can make the decision; he is a *disinterested* observer.

... **uninterested:** not interested at all

Jack is *uninterested* in checkers and never plays at all.

126. DONE

... **done:** Use only with "have," "has," or "had."

Done is the past participle of **do** (do, did, done). See 41-d.

Wrong: Bill *done* his homework.
Right: Bill *did* his homework. (past tense)
or: Bill *has done* his homework. (present perfect)
or: Bill *had done* his homework. (past perfect)

127. DON'T—DOESN'T

... **don't:** contraction meaning "do not"; use with all persons except third person, singular

> *I don't* enjoy large parties. (1st person)
> *You don't* have to shout. (2nd person)
> *They don't* plant tomatoes or beans. (3rd person, plural)
>
> *Not*: He, she, or it don't. (3rd person, singular)

... **doesn't:** contraction meaning "does not"; use only with third person, singular

> *Jim doesn't* want to go to the party.
> *It doesn't* make sense to do it that way.
>
> *Not*: I, you, we, or they doesn't.

128. EACH OTHER—ONE ANOTHER

... **each other:** Use when only two people are involved.

> Jack and Mindy talked with *each other*.

... **one another:** Use when more than two people are involved.

> Jack, Mindy, and Tom talked with *one another*.

129. ELIGIBLE—ILLEGIBLE

... **eligible:** qualified to be chosen; worthy to be chosen

> She is *eligible* to enter the contest.
> He is an *eligible* young bachelor.

... **illegible:** not legible; not readable

> Since his handwriting is *illegible*, his teacher cannot grade his essay.

130. EMIGRANT—IMMIGRANT; MIGRATE—MIGRANT

. . . **emigrant:**   one who leaves one country in order to live in another

> Several boatloads of *emigrants* from South Korea set sail for the U.S.

. . . **immigrant:**   one who enters a new country with the intention of taking up permanent residence

> Antonia, who was born in Poland, is a recent *immigrant*.

. . . **migrate:**   to travel from one place to another

> Every February the gray whales *migrate* from the Bering Sea to the Mexican coast.

. . . **migrant:**   a farm laborer who moves from place to place to harvest crops

> After several long, hungry days, the *migrants* found temporary work in San Diego, California.

12-5-94

131. EMINENT—IMMINENT

. . . **eminent:**   well-known; famous

> An *eminent* teacher once told me that a book shut tight is only a block of paper.

. . . **imminent:**   threatening in the immediate future

> We could tell by the black clouds that a storm was *imminent*.

132. ENVELOP—ENVELOPE

. . . **envelop:**   (accent on second syllable) a verb meaning "to wrap"
> *Envelop* the baby in this blanket.

. . . **envelope:**   (accent on first syllable) a noun meaning "a flat, paper container for a letter"
> He placed the valentine in the *envelope* and mailed it.

133. EVERYDAY—EVERY DAY

. . . **everyday:**   an adjective meaning "common," "usual"
Jumping from helicopters is an *everyday* experience for him.

. . . **every day:**   an adjective-noun combination meaning "day after day"
Her son does his homework *every day*.

134. EVERYONE—EVERY ONE

. . . **everyone:**   indefinite pronoun that always refers to a person
Everyone knows that an intersection is the meeting place of headlights and light heads!

. . . **every one:**   adjective-pronoun combination that can refer to a person or a thing
Every one of the psychiatrists agreed that a person with inhibitions is tied up in "nots"!

Every one of the flowers at the entrance to Disneyland is replaced seven times a year.

135. FARTHER—FURTHER

. . . **farther:**   measures physical distance only
My house is five miles *farther* from school than your house is.

. . . **further:**   measures non-physical distance
Jim is *further* in his studies than Max.

136. FEWER—LESS

. . . **fewer:**   a noun or modifier of a noun that can be counted
A human has *fewer* wisdom teeth than an elephant. (A human has four; an elephant has 24!)

. . . **less:**   a noun or modifer of a noun that can't be counted
But the elephant has *less* wisdom than a human—probably!

137. FIRSTLY

. . . Avoid using **firstly** at all. Use "first."

138. FORMALLY—FORMERLY

. . . **formally:** established by custom or rule

For the prom, he was *formally* dressed in a tuxedo.

She was *formally* addressed as president by the members of the committee.

. . . **formerly:** earlier in time

This man, *formerly* called Sam Smith, is now known as Sam Spade.

139. -FUL—FULL

. . . **-ful:** the correct adjective ending

beauti*ful*—merci*ful*—bounti*ful*

. . . **full:** used only as a separate word

Jackie is *full* of ideas.

That box is *full* of junk.

140. GONE

. . . **gone:** Use only with "have," "has," or "had."

Gone is the past participle of **go** (go, went, gone).

Wrong: José *gone* to the store.
Right: José *went* to the store. (past tense)
or: José *has gone* to the store. (present perfect)
or: José *had gone* to the store. (past perfect)

141. GOOD—WELL

. . . **good:** always an adjective

Isabel is a *good* skater.
Isabel looks *good*. (meaning "attractive")
Isabel feels *good*. (meaning "happy")

Laugh Your Way Through Grammar

... **well:**   usually an adverb

>   Isabel skates *well*. (adverb)

but an adjective when used to refer to health

>   Isabel feels *well*. (adjective, describing her health)

>   Note: She is *good*.   (has a good nature, is moral)
>   She is *well*.   (is healthy)

Both sentences are correct, but they have different meanings.

142. GORILLA—GUERRILLA

... **gorilla:**   noun meaning "an anthropoid ape"

>   Tarzan chatted with the *gorillas* in the trees.

... **guerrilla:**   noun or adjective referring to one who engages in irregular warfare

>   The secret activities of the *guerrillas* were hampered by the curiosity of the friendly *gorillas*.

143. GOT

... **got:**   Do not use unnecessarily with "have," "has," or "had."

Wrong: The aardvark *has got* a sticky tongue that is a foot and a half long.
Right: The aardvark *has* a sticky tongue that is a foot and a half long.

Wrong: They *have got* a new definition for violinist: someone up to the chin in music.
Right: They *have* a new definition for violinist: someone up to the chin in music.

144. GRADUATE—GRADUATE FROM

. . . If the verb **graduate** precedes an institution, the preposition **from** must be used.

Wrong: After *graduating* high school, Jesse joined the Marines.

Right: After *graduating from* high school, Jesse joined the Marines.

Wrong: Jesse *graduated* Merrydale High School in 1988.

Right: Jesse *graduated from* Merrydale High School in 1988.

145. HAD OUGHT

. . . **had ought:** Always incorrect.

Wrong: A grapefruit *had ought* to be described as a popular eye tonic.

Right: A grapefruit *ought* to be described as a popular eye tonic.

146. HANGED—HUNG

. . . **hanged:** used to describe the execution of a person

The murderer was *hanged* because he had committed a capital offense.

. . . **hung:** used to describe things that are suspended

The picture was *hung* on the north wall.
Mary *hung* her coat on the coatrack.

147. HEALTHY—HEALTHFUL

. . . **healthy:** indicates good physical condition

People are *healthy*.
Animals are *healthy*.

. . . **healthful:** indicates something that leads to good health

Spinach is a *healthful* food.
Exercise in moderation is *healthful*.

Laugh Your Way Through Grammar

148. HISTORIC—HISTORICAL

. . . **historic:**   important as a part of history

The Capitol is a *historic* building.

Many *historic* landmarks are being preserved and even restored.

. . . **historical:**   based on a special period in history

John Jakes writes *historical* novels.

He collected the *historical* facts about the Boston Massacre before he developed his own theory as to its results.

149. HOPEFULLY

. . . **hopefully:**   an adverb meaning "in a hopeful manner"; it cannot mean "we hope" or "it is hoped"

Right: Christine is working *hopefully* for a scholarship.

Wrong: *Hopefully*, the two countries will not go to war.

Right: It is *hoped* that the two countries will not go to war.

It is best not to use *hopefully* at all, since it is often used incorrectly.

150. IMPLY—INFER

. . . **imply:**   to hint; to suggest

When Zach said that about 17,000 distinctive smells have been classified, he was *implying* that he is an expert on odors.

. . . **infer:**   to conclude

When Zach said that about 17,000 distinctive smells have been classified, we *inferred* that he is an expert on odors.

Problem Words and Expressions

151. IN—INTO

   . . . **in:**   means "inside"

                   Bert is *in* the drawing room.

   . . . **into:**   is used to indicate the act of "entering"

                   Bert is going *into* the drawing room.

152. INSIDE OF

   . . . **inside of:**   Do not use **inside of** for **within**.

                   Wrong: She built the hut *inside of* a week.
                   Right: She built the hut *within* a week.

   . . . **inside of:**   Do not use **inside of** for **inside**.

                   Wrong: Stay *inside of* the amusement park.
                   Right: Stay *inside* the amusement park.

153. IRREGARDLESS

   . . . **irregardless:**   Always wrong.

                   Wrong: He went *irregardless* of his mother's warning.
                   Right: He went *regardless* of his mother's warning.

154. IS BECAUSE, IS WHEN, IS WHERE, IS WHY

   . . . Never use an adverbial clause after any form of the verb "to be."

Wrong: His anger *is because* he is suffering.
Right: His anger is due to his suffering.
or: He is angry because he is suffering.

Wrong: Inflation *is when* wallets are getting bigger and shopping bags are getting smaller.
Right: Inflation is a time when wallets are getting bigger and shopping bags are getting smaller.
or: Inflation usually means that wallets are getting bigger and shopping bags are getting smaller.

                                   Laugh Your Way Through Grammar

Wrong: Matt's Club *is where* the action is.
Right: Matt's Club is the place where the action is.
or: Matt's Club is the scene of the action.

Wrong: Politicians are often in hot water; *that's why* they sometimes get hardboiled!
Right: Politicians are often in hot water; that's the reason they sometimes get hardboiled!
or: Because politicians are often in hot water, they sometimes get hardboiled!

155. IT

. . . **It** must have an antecedent: a specific word to which **it** refers. Do not try to make **it** refer to an entire clause.

> Wrong: When you feel yourself turning green with envy, *it* means you're ripe for trouble.
> Right: When you feel yourself turning green with envy, you're ripe for trouble.

156. KIND OF A, SORT OF A, TYPE OF A

. . . Do not use the article **a** or **an** after **kind of**, **sort of**, and **type of**.

> Wrong: What *kind of a* driver never gets arrested?
> Right: What *kind of* driver never gets arrested? (a screwdriver)

157. KINDS

. . . The plural **kinds** must be used after "two" or more.

> Wrong: two *kind* of *oranges*
> Right: two *kinds* of *oranges*
>
> Wrong: several *kind* of *oranges*
> Right: several *kinds* of *oranges*

158. LATER—LATTER

. . . **later:**   comparative form of the adjective **late**

Luis came late, but Jack came even *later*.

. . . **latter:**   relating to the second of two persons or things

You can study in the morning or you can study now, but the *latter* is preferable.

159. LAY—LIE

. . . **lay:**   means to place, to put; a transitive verb (always takes an object)

Principal parts: lay, laid, (have, has, had) laid

I *lay* the book on the table.
("book"—direct object)
Yesterday he *laid* the book on the table.
He *has laid* a book on the table every day this week.

(If you mentally replace each italicized verb with "put" and the sentence makes sense, then you know that some form of **lay** is the correct verb.)

. . . **lie:**   means to recline, to stretch out; an intransitive verb (never takes an object)

Principal parts: lie, lay, (have, has, had) lain

He *lies* on the bed every day at two.
Yesterday she *lay* on the bed.
That book *has lain* on the table for three days.

160. LAYING—LYING

. . . **laying:**   the present participle of **lay**

I am *laying* (putting, placing) the book on the table.

. . . **lying:**   the present participle of **lie**

He is *lying* (reclining) on the bed.

Laugh Your Way Through Grammar

161. LEARN—TEACH

. . . **learn:**   to acquire information or a skill
I am *learning* Spanish.
I have *learned* to type.

. . . **teach:**   to impart or give information or a skill
My brother will *teach* me Spanish.
My brother *taught* me to type.

162. LEAVE—LET

. . . **leave:**   means "to go away"; "to abandon"
Please *leave* me now. (go away)

. . . **let:**   means "to allow"; "not to disturb"
Please *let* me alone. (don't disturb me)
Please *let* me write that story for the paper. (allow me to)

Notice that **let** functions as an *auxiliary* verb while **leave** never does. Hence . . .

Let's go to the game.   *Let* me walk alone.

163. LEND—LOAN—BORROW

. . . **lend:**   a verb meaning "to let someone have something on condition it be returned"
I promised to *lend* him $100.

. . . **loan:**   a noun meaning "something lent"
I obtained a *loan* of $100.

. . . **borrow:**   a verb meaning "to receive something with the understanding that one will return it"
I would like to *borrow* $100.

164. LIABLE—LIKELY

. . . **liable:**   expresses an unpleasant possibility
If you walk on ice, you are *liable* to fall.

. . . **likely:**   expresses possibility
Katrina is *likely* to be elected.

165. LIKE—AS—AS IF

. . . **like:** can be a preposition, but never a conjunction

Wrong: They are acting *as* children.
Right: They are acting *like children.*
    ("like children"—prepositional phrase)

Wrong: "Nobody can do it *like* McDonald's can."
Right: "Nobody can do it *as McDonald's can.*"
    ("as McDonald's can"—clause)

Wrong: She said it *like* she meant it.
Right: She said it *as if she meant it.*
    ("as if she meant it"—clause)

166. LOOSE—LOSE

. . . **loose:** adjective meaning "not tight"

"*Loose* lips sink ships!" (World War II slogan)

. . . **lose:** verb meaning "to misplace"; "to fail to keep"

If you *lose* an hour in the morning, you will chase it all the day.

167. MAJORITY—PLURALITY

. . . **majority:** Means more than half. If **majority** refers to a specific number, it takes a singular verb.

Melanie's *majority was* three votes.

If **majority** refers to the individual members of a group, it takes a plural verb.

A *majority* of the team *are* going to Miami.

. . . **plurality:** Means more than anyone else received, but not necessarily more than half.

He won with a *plurality* of three votes.

Although she received a *plurality* of the votes cast, she did not receive the majority needed for election.

168. MAY—MIGHT

... **may:**   expresses a possibility

> I *may* go to college next fall.

... **might:**   expresses a possibility but with more doubt

> I *might* go to college next fall.

169. MAY BE—MAYBE

... **maybe:**   adverb meaning ''perhaps''

> *Maybe* a compulsive golfer should be called a crackputt!

... **may be:**   verb phrase

> The abdomen *may be called* the Department of the Interior!

Easy Aid: If you're in doubt, substitute the word ''perhaps.'' If it works, use ''maybe'' (one word); if it doesn't, use ''may be'' (two words).

170. MORAL—MORALE

... **moral:**   noun or adjective indicating proper behavior

> Sue's *moral* code prevented her from lying.
> (''moral''—adjective modifying ''code'')

> Jamie's *morals* are based on the precept: ''Do unto others as you would have others do unto you.''
> (''morals''—noun, subject of ''are based'')

... **morale:**   noun meaning ''general attitude'' and ''outlook''

> Jess' *morale* is high, and he has a good chance of winning the contest.
> (''morale''—noun, subject of ''is'')

171. NOT ONLY . . . BUT ALSO

. . . The **not only** phrase must form a parallel construction to the **but also** phrase: that is, if a *verb* follows **not only,** a *verb* must follow **but also;** if a *noun* follows **not only,** a *noun* must follow **but also.**

Wrong: An octopus not only has eight legs but also blue blood.

Right: An octopus not only has eight legs but also has blue blood.

Right: An octopus has not only eight legs but also blue blood.

172. NOTORIOUS—FAMOUS

. . . **notorious:**   well-known in an unsavory way

Al Capone was a *notorious* gangster.

. . . **famous:**   well-known in a favorable way

The *famous* Albert Einstein was a mathematical genius.

173. NUMBERS

. . . Spell out all numbers from one through ninety-nine as well as other numbers written as one word; for example, hundred, thousand, etc. Use Arabic numerals for the others.

I own *three* cats and *twenty* mice.
There are 990,000 people who own *300* books.

See also 239, numbers.

174. PAIR

. . . **a pair:**   a noun meaning "a single thing with two parts that are used together"; takes a singular verb

A pair of scissors *is* lying on the table.

. . . **two pairs:**   takes a plural verb

Two pairs of scissors *are* lying on the table.

Laugh Your Way Through Grammar

. . . **A pair** (referring to two individuals) takes a plural verb.

The pair of them *are* going to Niagara Falls.

175. PART FROM—PART WITH

. . . **part from:**   Use with a person.

I hate to *part from* my cousin.

. . . **part with:**   Use with a thing.

I hate to *part with* my good-luck charm.

12-12

176. PASSED—PAST

. . . **passed:**   a verb meaning "went by"; "approved"

Gina *passed* that store every day for a month.
In 1457, in Scotland, a law was *passed* making it illegal to play golf.

. . . **past:**   a preposition, an adjective, an adverb, or a noun

(1) Ellie is *past* the age for playing with dolls.
(preposition; *age* its object)

(2) For the *past* few days, Ellie has been depressed.
(adjective; modifying *days*)

(3) Frank waved as he walked *past*.
(adverb; modifying *walked*)

(4) In the *past*, I sometimes worried about unimportant things.
(noun; object of the preposition *in*)

177. PEACE—PIECE

. . . **peace:**   a state of quiet; freedom from disturbance

During the past 4,000 years, there have been fewer than 300 years of *peace*.

. . . **piece:**   a part of a whole

"It's a *piece* of cake!" he said sweetly as he broke the world's dessert-eating record.

178. PERSONAL—PERSONNEL

... **personal:** relating to a person; private

He bought the company for *personal* financial gain.

... **personnel:** a body of persons employed by a particular firm; may take a singular or a plural verb

Our personnel *is* made up of former farmers.

Our personnel *are* voting today on rules governing retirement.

179. PRAY—PREY

... **pray:** a verb meaning "to plead," "to entreat"

Kit *prayed* that she would be rescued.

... **prey:** a verb meaning "to seize and devour"; "to injure"

The owl *preys* on small animals and birds.

... **prey:** a noun meaning "an animal seized for food; a victim"

The eagle is a bird of *prey*.
(The eagle does the seizing.)

The rabbit is often *prey* to the owl.
(The rabbit is the victim.)

Zeke is a *prey* to his own greed.
(Zeke is the victim.)

180. PRINCIPAL—PRINCIPLE

... **principal:** the head person or the major item

Make a PAL of your *princiPAL*.

The *princiPAL* reason for his failure is that he didn't study.

... **principle:** a ruLE or a truth

He lives by the *principLE* that honesty is the best policy.

181. PROPHECY—PROPHESY

. . . **prophecy:** (The "cy" ending is pronounced "see.") noun meaning "a prediction of something to come"

Kate's *prophecy*—that her happiness would last only one week—came true.

. . . **prophesy:** (The "sy" ending is pronounced "sigh.") verb meaning "to predict something that is to come"

Did Kate *prophesy* the endless rain we've had?

Kate *prophesied* the endless rain we're now having.

182. QUIET—QUITE

. . . **quiet:** without noise or motion

Half of wisdom is keeping *quiet* when you have nothing to say.

A *quiet* tongue makes no enemies.

. . . **quite:** to a considerable extent

The family that chews gum together *quite* often sticks together!

Silly Suzy was *quite* certain that steel wool is the fleece from a hydraulic ram!

183. RAISE—RISE

. . . **raise:** means "to lift higher"; a transitive verb (always takes an object)

Principal parts: raise, raised, (have, has, had) raised

Maxine *raises* the flag every day.

Maxine *raised* the flag in front of the school.

Maxine *has raised* the flag in front of the school every day for a month.

Problem Words and Expressions   **185**

... **rise:**   means "to move upward"; an intransitive verb (never takes an object)

Principal parts: rise, rose, (have, has, had) risen

The sun *rises* at 6 a.m.

Maxine *rose* from the chair and went to work.

The boys *have risen* every day at 5 a.m.

184. REAL—REALLY

... **real:**   an adjective meaning "genuine"

That is a *real* diamond.
This is a *real* adventure.

... **really:**   an adverb meaning "truly" or "actually"

I *really* don't know the answer.
That is a *really* beautiful diamond.

185. in REGARD, in REGARDS TO

... When used with **in** or **with,** the singular form, **regard,** is always used.

Wrong: I am writing *in regards to* your letter.
Right: I am writing *in regard to* your letter.

186. SEEN

... **seen:**   Use only with "have," "has," or "had."

Seen is the past participle of **see** (see, saw, seen). See 41-d.

Wrong: Norm *seen* this license plate: EZ2PLEZ.
Right: Norm *saw* this license plate: EZ2PLEZ. (past)
or: Norm *has seen* this license plate: EZ2PLEZ. (present perfect)
or: Norm *had seen* this license plate: EZ2PLEZ. (past perfect)

187. SET—SIT

. . . **set:** means "to place in position, to put down"; a transitive verb (always takes an object)

Principal parts: set, set, set
Please *set* the book on the table.

Exceptions: Idiomatic uses of **set:**
The sun *sets* in the west.
Do you think the cement *has set*?

. . . **sit:** means "to take a seated position"; an intransitive verb (never takes an object)

Principal parts: sit, sat, sat
Please *sit* down.
She *sat* in the new chair.

188. SLOW—SLOWLY

. . . **slow:** an adjective
He is a *slow* starter.

. . . **slowly:** an adverb
She walked *slowly* down the steet.

Exception: Drive *slow*. (a permissible idiom)

189. SOME—SOMEWHAT

. . . Do not use **some** instead of **somewhat** as an adverb.
Wrong: Jake felt *some* better in the morning.
Right: Jake felt *somewhat* better in the morning.

(Note: If you can replace **some** with **rather,** use **somewhat.**)

190. STATIONARY—STATIONERY

. . . **stationAry:** stAnding in one place
The desk is stationAry. (It can't be moved.)

. . . **stationEry:** pEns, pEncils, and other writing supplies
He went to the stationEry store to buy stationEry.

191. STAYED—STOOD

. . . Do not use **stood** when you mean **stayed.** (Note: If you can substitute **remained,** use **stayed.**)
Wrong: She *stood* in bed.
Right: She *stayed* in bed.

192. SURE—SURELY

. . . **sure:**   an adjective
He is *sure* that he will pass.
It is a *sure* thing.

. . . **surely:**   an adverb
Katrina is *surely* happy about the results.
They *surely* ski like experts.

193. SURE AND, TRY AND—SURE TO, TRY TO

. . . Do not use **sure and** and **try and.** Use **sure to** and **try to.**
Wrong: Be *sure and* remind him that there has been only one indispensable man: Adam!
Right: Be *sure to* remind him that there has been only one indispensable man: Adam!

Wrong: Sheila told her husband she would *try and* buy a car with power steering for backseat drivers.
Right: Sheila told her husband she would *try to* buy a car with power steering for backseat drivers.

194. THEIR—THERE—THEY'RE

. . . **their:**   possessive adjective
They lost *their* jackets.

. . . **there:**   adverb indicating place
He sat in the bleachers and left his jacket *there.*

. . . **they're:**   contraction meaning "they are"
They're sure that even Joshua couldn't make the modern "son" stand still!

195. THEN—THAN

. . . **then:** an adverb denoting time
He studied; *then* he went home.

. . . **than:** a conjunction suggesting comparison
It is better to wear out *than* to rust out.

196. THIS, THAT, THESE, THOSE with HERE or THERE

. . . Never use **here** or **there** after **this, that, these,** or **those.**

Wrong: this *here* tomato
Right: this tomato

Wrong: that *there* tomato
Right: that tomato

197. THIS, THAT, THESE, THOSE with KIND(s), SORT(s), TYPE(s)

. . . **this** and **that:** always singular
. . . **these** and **those:** always plural

Right: this (that) *kind* of *tomato* or *tomatoes*
Right: these (those) *kinds* of *tomatoes*

Right: this (that) *type* of *student*
Right: these (those) *types* of *students*

198. TO—TOO—TWO

. . . **to:** preposition; introduces a prepositional phrase
Three of every four visitors *to Walt Disney World* are adults.

. . . **too:** also; more than enough
A man is never *too* old to learn, but he is sometimes *too* young.

. . . **two:** the number 2
For every child who turns sixteen, *two* adults turn pale.

Problem Words and Expressions

189

199. UP (as an unnecessary word)

. . . Avoid using **up** unnecessarily.

> Wrong: Silly Suzy opened *up* a box of crackers to celebrate the Fourth of July.
> Right: Silly Suzy opened a box of crackers to celebrate the Fourth of July.

> Wrong: Please close *up* the door.
> Right: Please close the door.

> Wrong: They washed *up* the dishes.
> Right: They washed the dishes.

200. USE TO—USED TO

. . . **Used to** is correct; **use to** is always incorrect.

> Wrong: She *use to* say that dieting is the triumph of mind over platter!
> Right: She *used to* say that dieting is the triumph of mind over platter!

201. WANT

. . . Certain uses of **want** are incorrect although they are used often in speech.

> Wrong: She *wants for you* to be ambitious.
> Right: She *wants you* to be ambitious.

> Wrong: She *wants you should be* ambitious.
> Right: She *wants you to be* ambitious.

> Wrong: She wants *in*.
> Right: She wants *to come in*.

> Wrong: She wants *out*.
> Right: She wants *to go out*.

202. WEATHER—WHETHER

. . . **weather:** condition of the atmosphere—heat or cold, rain or sun, etc.

The one person who's always wrong yet never fired is the *weather* forecaster.

. . . **whether:** usually used with "or" to express a choice of alternatives (the "or" may be implied or stated)

I couldn't decide *whether* Europe *or* Africa would be my first choice for my vacation.

I couldn't decide *whether* Europe would be my first choice for my vacation.

203. WHO (WHOM)—WHICH—THAT

. . . **who (whom):** refers to a person

. . . **which:** refers to an animal, or an inanimate object

. . . **that:** refers to a person or to an inanimate object

If a vegetarian is someone *who* (*that*) eats vegetables, what is a humanitarian?

The roller coaster, *which* probably had its origin in the ice slides of 15th-century Russia, is a popular amusement park ride.

204. WHO'S—WHOSE

. . . **who's:** a contraction meaning "who is"

Tim is the one *who's* insisting that an alarm clock is something that scares the daylight into you!

Who's going to insist that the hen is immortal because her "son" never sets?

... **whose:**   a possessive pronoun

> *Whose* words are these: "Heavier-than-air flying machines are impossible"? (Lord Kelvin, in 1895)

> **Easy Aid:** When in doubt, substitute "who is." If it works, use **who's.** If it doesn't, use **whose.**

WHO (WHOM)—WHOSE. For a further study, see 37-f.

205. YOU'RE—YOUR

... **you're:**   a contraction meaning "you are"

> If *you're* not afraid to face the music, you may someday lead the band.

... **your:**   a possessive adjective

> Do you have *your* checkbook with you?

> **Easy Aid:** When in doubt, substitute "you are." If it works, use **you're.** If it doesn't, use **your.**

SECTION V

Capitalization, Punctuation, Spelling—And Other Matters

CAPITALIZATION

PUNCTUATION

Continued on Following Page

CAPITALIZATION

206. Capitalize the pronoun **I** and the interjection **O,** but *not* the interjection **oh.**

> He said that I might go.
> "But O for the touch of a vanish'd hand . . . "
> "I'm happy, oh, so happy!" she cried.

207. Capitalize the first word of every sentence.

> The giraffe nibbled on the leaves.

208. Capitalize the first word of every line of poetry.

> "Is this a dagger which I see before me,
> The handle toward my hand? Come, let me clutch thee."
>
> Shakespeare—*Macbeth*

209. QUOTATIONS

a. Capitalize the first word of a direct quotation.

> He said, "The Grand Canyon is incredibly beautiful."

b. Do *not* capitalize the second half of a split quotation.

> "The Grand Canyon," he said, "is incredibly beautiful."

c. Do *not* capitalize a piece of a quotation.

> He used the words "incredibly beautiful" to describe the Grand Canyon.

d. Do *not* capitalize an indirect quotation.

> He said that the Grand Canyon is incredibly beautiful.

210. PROPER NOUNS AND PROPER ADJECTIVES

a. (1) Capitalize proper nouns and proper adjectives.

PROPER NOUN	PROPER ADJECTIVE
Shakespeare	Shakespearean poetry
Ireland	Irish philosophy
France	French dressing

(2) Capitalize the initials that are part of a proper noun.

J. P. Morgan
John D. Rockefeller

(3) Capitalize all nationalities, languages, and races.

Caucasian
Semitic
Belgian
Italian
Spanish

(4) Do *not* capitalize the prefix of a proper adjective.

anti-Russian   pro-French
un-American   pre-Columbian

b. Capitalize names of ships, trains, planes, cars, specific buildings, etc.

the Mississippi Queen   (ship)
the Santa Fe Limited   (train)
Air Force One   (plane)
the Trade Center   (building)

c. Capitalize historic events, periods, and documents.

the Battle of Bunker Hill   the Twenties
the Bill of Rights   the Middle Ages
the War of 1812   World War II

d. Capitalize names of days, months, holidays, and calendar events.

Tuesday	August
Fourth of July	Thanksgiving
Secretary's Week	Lent

Do *not* capitalize seasons: summer, winter, spring, fall, and autumn.

211. GEOGRAPHICAL TERMS

a. Capitalize geographical proper nouns.

New York City	(but—the city of New York)
Mississippi River	(but—a river in Mississippi)
Warren County	(but—the county of Warren)
Pacific Ocean	(but—an ocean)

Others: Boulder Dam; Fifth Avenue; Adirondack Mountains; Grand Canyon; Niagara Falls; North America; Lake Erie; the Dead Sea; the United States of America (Notice that "the" and "of" are not capitalized.)

b. Capitalize the first part of a hyphenated street name—but *not* the second part.

Forty-second Street
Thirty-fourth Street

c. Do *not* capitalize points of the compass, but do capitalize these terms when they name parts of the country.

He traveled north on Route 1.
He lives in the North.

They drove southwest to Phoenix.
They settled in the Southwest.

Massachusetts is east of San Francisco.
Massachusetts is in the East; San Francisco is in the West.

212. ORGANIZATIONS

a. Capitalize names of all organizations and institutions.

Sears, Roebuck & Company	Library of Congress
Boy Scouts of America	Lions Club
Chamber of Commerce	Photography Club
Democratic Party	Republican Party

b. Capitalize words denoting members of an organization.

the Boy Scouts	the Lions
the Democrats	the Republicans

c. Capitalize brand names but *not* the common nouns that follow them.

Ansco camera	Ford cars
Pillsbury biscuits	Johnson's baby powder

213. EDUCATIONAL TERMS

a. Capitalize names of particular schools and colleges.

In Merrydale High School, the dictionary is the only place where success comes before work.

BUT: In our high school, the dictionary is the only place where success comes before work.

He attended the University of Texas in Austin.

BUT: He attended college in Austin, Texas.

b. Capitalize specific courses, usually numbered, and language courses.

She is studying Biology II this year. (numbered)

BUT: She is studying biology this year.

He is studying French this year.   (language)

c. Do not capitalize names of classes.

> She is a senior.
> He is a sophomore.

214. RELIGIOUS TERMS

a. Capitalize names of religions whether used as nouns or adjectives.

Protestant	the Protestant belief
Jewish	the Judaic law
Catholic	the Catholic creed

Capitalize the names of religious congregations.

| Protestants | Catholics |
| Jews | Presbyterians |

b. Capitalize the word **God** and titles and pronouns that substitute for **God.** (Exception: do not capitalize the word "gods" when referring to ancient deities.)

> He studied the word of God daily.
> When God created the world, He did it in six days.
> He appealed to his Savior for help.

c. Capitalize the word **Bible** and all books of the Bible.

> She read the Bible daily.
> Her favorite book of the Bible was Genesis.
> She studied the Scriptures in college.

215. TITLES

a. Capitalize family titles when they are part of a name. Do *not* capitalize if a pronoun immediately precedes the title.

	That's Uncle Sam.
BUT:	That is my uncle.

	I asked Mother if I could go.
BUT:	I asked my mother if I could go.

	We visited Cousin Emma for one week.
BUT:	We visited our cousin Emma for one week.

b. Capitalize other titles when they are part of a name.

	I called Senator Smith about the problem.
BUT:	I called my senator about the problem.

	Dr. Joan Smith said that the only exercise some patients get is stretching the truth!
BUT:	One doctor said that the only exercise some patients get is stretching the truth!

	I know Judge O'Connor very well.
BUT:	My friend is a judge on the Family Court.

	He was the president of the senior class.
BUT:	He was the President of the United States.
OR:	He was President Ronald Reagan.

(The word **president** when it refers to a President of a nation is always capitalized.)

Others:	Mayor Carol Smith (but—the mayor of Merrydale)
	Captain Fred Allen (but—a captain in the Air Force)
	Principal Mike Trent (but—a principal of a school)

Laugh Your Way Through Grammar

Note: *Vice President* is used when referring to the official of a nation; but—a student may be the *vice-president* of his class.

He is an ex-President. ("ex" not capitalized)
She is Governor-elect. ("elect" not capitalized)

c. Capitalize a title that takes the place of a name in direct address.

Please understand, *Senator*, that procrastination is the fertilizer that makes difficulties grow!

"Tell me, *Captain*, are we in immediate danger?"

216. PUBLICATIONS

a. In the names of magazines and newspapers, capitalize all words except articles, conjunctions, and prepositions unless one of these words begins the name.

The New York Times   *Sports Illustrated*

b. In the titles of books, poems, movies, works of art, etc., capitalize all words except articles, conjunctions, and prepositions unless one of these words begins the title. (Exceptions: Prepositions of four or more letters are usually capitalized.) All forms of the verb *be* (*is, are, am*, etc.) are always capitalized.

Of Human Bondage (novel by Somerset Maugham)
A Tale of Two Cities (novel by Charles Dickens)
"The Star-Spangled Banner" (song by Francis Scott Key)
"The Masque of the Red Death" (poem by E. A. Poe)
Woman With Book (painting by Pablo Picasso)
"This Is Your Life" (TV show)

217. OTHERS

a. After a colon, capitalize a long statement but not a short one.

He didn't want to go: he had to study.
He didn't want to go: He had an exam scheduled in three days, an important exam, and he had to pass it with a high grade if he hoped to be admitted to law school.

b. Capitalize the first word after ''Resolved.''

Resolved, That the seniors will earn enough money to pay for a trip to Washington, D.C.

218. ABBREVIATIONS

Capitalize many—but not all—abbreviations.

a. Always capitalized:

2001 B.C.   A.D. 2001
(Notice that **B.C.** follows the date,
while **A.D.** precedes the date.)
Jr. (Junior) as in John Smith, Jr.
Sr. (Senior) as in John Smith, Sr.
Vt. (Vermont), L.A. (Los Angeles)
Feb. (February), Wed. (Wednesday)

b. Sometimes capitalized (optional):

a.m. or A.M.   p.m. or P.M.

c. *Never* capitalized:

v. or vs. (opposed to)   e.g. (for example)

(When in doubt, consult any dictionary.)

219. SALUTATION AND COMPLIMENTARY CLOSING OF LETTERS

a. Capitalize all important words of the salutation.

Dear Sir: My dear Madam:
Dear Mr. President: Dear Ms. Edison: (or Mrs. or Miss)

b. Capitalize the first word of the complimentary closing.

Very truly yours,   Yours truly,
Sincerely yours,   Yours respectfully,

PUNCTUATION

220. PERIOD

A **period** indicates a full stop.

a. A period is used at the end of every declarative and imperative sentence.

> A dietitian is someone who lives on the fat of the land. (declarative)
> Go home now.   (imperative)

b. A period is used after most abbreviations and initials.

> T.S. Eliot   Pa. (Pennsylvania)
> Harry S. Truman   Dec. (December)

However, some often-used abbreviations are not followed by periods:

> UN (United Nations); FHA (Federal Housing Authority)

c. A period is placed inside end quotation marks.

> The speaker added, "Humor is the hole that lets the sawdust out of a stuffed shirt."

> Cyril Connolly called sculpture "mud pies which endure."

d. Three periods . . . (called an ellipsis mark) indicate the omission of some words of text. Use four periods if the ellipsis ends the sentence.

Original quotation: "Nothing short of independence, it appears to me, can possibly do. A peace on other terms would, if I may be allowed the expression, be a peace of war." (George Washington)

Shortened quotation: "Nothing short of independence . . . can possibly do. A peace on other terms would . . . be a peace of war."

221. QUESTION MARK

A **question mark** is placed at the end of every question. It may also suggest doubt.

a. A question mark should be used at the end of a question.

How can you take five strokes off your golf game? (Use an eraser!)
What is a credit card? (A BUY pass!)

b. A question mark is used after a parenthetical question.

When you study (you will, won't you?), remember to take detailed notes.

c. A question mark should be placed INSIDE the end quotation mark if it applies to the quotation only.

I asked, ''Why does she call her desk a wastebasket with drawers?''

BUT: A question mark should be placed OUTSIDE the end quotation mark if it applies to the whole sentence.

Did you realize I was one of the ''Terrible Thirteen''?

d. A question mark in parentheses (?) may be used to indicate uncertainty.

Lea was born at 5 a.m. (?) last Sunday.

222. SEMICOLON

A **semicolon** indicates a strong pause.

a. A semicolon is used between two closely related independent clauses that are *not* connected by a conjunction.

> Don't tell a secret in the barn; horses carry "tails."
>
> Experience is a hard teacher; she tests first—and teaches afterward.

b. A semicolon is used between two independent clauses connected by a *conjunctive adverb* (74), or by an explanatory word or phrase. A comma commonly follows a conjunctive adverb.

however	nevertheless	therefore	thus
for instance	otherwise	instead	hence
consequently	for example	then	so

> He was always at the foot of his class; consequently, he decided to become a chiropodist.

c. A semicolon is used for clarity if a sentence contains a number of commas.

> He invited Ellie, the class clown; Trudy, the class wit; and Tom, the class gadfly.
>
> We went to Paris, France, on July 1, 1988; and we returned to Los Angeles, California, on August 3, 1988.
>
> Jan requested a meeting with Tom Jones, the president; Claire Smith, the vice-president; Martin Gaylord, the secretary; and Charity Black, the treasurer.

d. A semicolon is always placed outside end quotation marks.

> John Wayne was often called "Duke"; this nickname was the result of his playing the role of a duke in a school play.

223. COLON

A **colon** means—"Note what follows."

a. A colon is used to introduce a series following a noun or the phrase "as follows."

> Tessa invited three students: Jack Block, Sara Quentin, and Allan Pierce.
>
> Tessa invited the following students: Jack Block, Sara Quentin, and Allan Pierce.

However, the colon does *not* usually follow a verb.

> Wrong: Tessa invited: Jack, Sara, and Allan.
> Right:　Tessa invited Jack, Sara, and Allan.

b. A colon is used to introduce a word, phrase, or clause that explains the meaning of the main clause in a sentence.

> "Motel" is a portmanteau word: a blending of "motor" and "hotel."
>
> To remember the five Great Lakes, remember the word HOMES: H is for Lake Huron, O for Lake Ontario, M for Lake Michigan, E for Lake Erie, and S for Lake Superior.

In sentences of this type, a colon instead of a semicolon (222-a) may be used to separate the independent clauses.

> My father makes faces all day: he works in a clock factory!
>
> My father makes faces all day; he works in a clock factory!

When in doubt, use the semicolon.

c. A colon is used to introduce a quotation.

> Lincoln began his Gettysburg Address with these words: "Fourscore and seven years ago."

d. A colon is used after the salutation of a business letter.

> Dear Madam:　　　　　Dear Sir:
> Dear Mr. Edwards:　　Dear Editor:

e. A colon is used—

. . . between the hour and the minute.

We left at 1:25 p.m.

. . . between chapter and verse of the Bible.

I read Genesis 1:4.
(Book of Genesis, Chapter 1, Verse 4)

224. COMMA

A **comma** indicates a brief pause.

a. A comma is used after each noun in a series.

Rosalie gave three examples of collective nouns: the dust-pan, the garbage pail, and the vacuum cleaner.

b. A comma is used after each predicate in a series.

Adam and Eve were good mathematicians: they added the devil, subtracted happiness, divided from God, and went forth to multiply.

c. (1) A comma is used after each adjective in a series.

Clare Booth Luce once said that politicians talk themselves "red, white, and blue in the face"!

(2) A comma is used between *two* consecutive adjectives in a series IF the word "and" could be used, instead.

Tabitha has a small, white kitten. (It is possible to say "small and white," so a comma is used.)

Tabitha has a small Angora kitten. (It would be unnatural to say "small and Angora," so a comma is not used.)

d. A comma is used after each short clause in a series.

> Julius Caesar said, "I came, I saw, I conquered."
> The kitten played with the ball: she pushed it, she scuffed it, she tore it apart.

e. A comma is used after each phrase or clause IF the phrases or clauses are strictly parallel.

> ". . . and that government of the people, by the people, for the people, shall not perish from the earth."

> "We hold these truths to be self-evident: that all men are created equal, that they are endowed by their Creator with certain unalienable rights, that among these are life, liberty, and the pursuit of happiness . . ."

> The Declaration of Independence states that George III had chosen to plunder our seas, to ravage our coasts, to burn our towns, and to destroy the lives of our people.

f. A comma is used between the independent clauses in a compound sentence (11-b).

> I cracked the nuts, and then I removed the meat.
> Tillie walked home, but Celia took the bus.

Note: A comma is *not* used between the parts of a compound predicate.

> I cracked the nuts and then removed the meat. (no comma— compound predicate)

g. A comma is used after an introductory dependent clause in a complex sentence (11-c).

> If you split your sides laughing, you should run until you get a stitch in them.
> When the stars get hungry, they take a bite of the Milky Way.

h. A comma is often used after an introductory prepositional phrase.

> To the teenager, home is merely a filling station.

i. A comma is used after a verbal or verbal phrase that introduces a sentence.

> (1) Whistling, we walked down the street.   (participle)

> (2) Whistling merrily, we walked down the street.
>   (participial phrase)

> (3) To perfect the process, we added a new acid.
>   (infinitive phrase)

However—a verbal that is the subject of a sentence is *not* separated by a comma from its predicate.

> Eating is a pleasant social event.   (gerund as subject)

> "To err is human."   (infinitive as subject)

j. A comma is used before and after a verbal or verbal phrase that appears in the middle of a sentence.

> The six boys, whistling merrily, walked down the street.
> (participial phrase)

> The scientists, to perfect the process, added a new acid.
> (infinitive phrase)

k. A comma is often used before a verbal that appears at the end of a sentence.

> Walking down the street were six boys, whistling merrily.

l. Commas should be used to separate nonessential (non-restrictive) clauses or phrases from the rest of the sentence. Commas are *not* used with essential (restrictive) clauses and phrases.

> Jim Brown, who lives on Owen Avenue, won the election.

> > ("Who lives on Owen Avenue" is not essential to the meaning of the sentence and therefore is separated by commas.)

> The boy who lives on Owen Avenue won the election.

> > ("Who lives on Owen Avenue," identifying "boy," is essential to the meaning of the sentence and therefore is *not* separated by commas.)

Sally, grinning happily, was declared the winner.
(nonessential participial phrase)
The girl grinning happily was declared the winner.
(essential participial phrase)

m. A comma is used before and after an appositive within a sentence. If an appositive ends the sentence, only one comma is used. (See 19.) If an appositive is a single word, its connection is usually too close to require commas for separation.

Amelia, a tall girl, went out for basketball.
The favorite in the one-mile race was Jed, a runner with several awards.
My sister Nancy is studying for the SAT.

n. A comma is used to set off words in direct address.

Angela, please come here.
Tell me, Mary, how you can carry water in a sieve. (Answer: first freeze the water!)

o. A comma is used after *yes*, *no*, *well*, *oh*, *why*, etc., at the beginning of a sentence. (See also 76.)

Yes, I would like to receive a copy of your book.
Well, perhaps I will go with you.
Oh, he frightened me!
Why, I hadn't even considered that possibility.

p. A comma is used before and after parenthetical expressions.

A prison warden is a person who, not surprisingly, makes a living by the pen!
"Old Blood and Guts" was, of course, a nickname for General George Patton.

q. A comma is used to separate items in dates and places.

He was born in Akron, Ohio, on Tuesday, July 12, 1837.

In a ZIP code, a comma is used between the city and the state but is *not* used between the initials of the state and the ZIP number, as below.

He sent the letter to his aunt in Radnor, PA 19088.

r. A comma is used to separate a quotation from the rest of the sentence.

"Never lend money; it gives people amnesia," said Fred.

Fred said, "Never lend money; it gives people amnesia."

In a broken quotation, the interrupter must be set off with two commas.

"Never lend money," said Fred, "because it gives people amnesia."

However—do *not* use a comma with an indirect quotation.

Fred said that we should go to the circus.

s. A comma is used WHENEVER NECESSARY to make the meaning clear.

Wrong: Outside the moon glittered on the snow.
Right: Outside, the moon glittered on the snow.

Wrong: If you want to study all night.
Right: If you want to, study all night.

Wrong: To Charles Elizabeth is more mother than queen.
Right: To Charles, Elizabeth is more mother than queen.

t. A comma is used to indicate that a word has been omitted.

Nina brought the spaghetti, and Jack, the sauce.

Jane owns a goldfish; Millie, a guppy.

u. A comma is used after the salutation of a friendly letter.

Dear Jack,   Dear Aunt Emily,

v. A comma is used after the complimentary closing of any letter, whether business or friendly.

Love,   Very truly yours,

As ever,   Yours sincerely,

w. A comma is used before and after degrees and titles.

> Elizabeth Hunter, Ph.D., is speaking today.
> That is John L. Davis, Jr., on the speaker's platform.

x. A comma is never used to separate a subject from a predicate.

> Wrong: The storm with its high winds and pelting rain, destroyed the town beach.
> Right: The storm with its high winds and pelting rain destroyed the town beach.
> Right: The storm, with its high winds and pelting rain, destroyed the town beach.

225. QUOTATION MARKS

a. Quotation marks are used to indicate the actual speech of someone.

> (1) "Excuse me while I disappear," said Frank Sinatra to some reporters.
> (2) Frank Sinatra said to some reporters, "Excuse me while I disappear."
> (3) "Excuse me," Frank Sinatra said to some reporters, "while I disappear."

When two sentences are quoted, the sentences may be punctuated in several ways.

> (4) Jane said, "I hurt my knee. It's bleeding!"
> (5) "I hurt my knee. It's bleeding!" Jane said.
> (6) "I hurt my knee," Jane said. "It's bleeding!"
> (7) "I hurt my knee," Jane said; "it's bleeding!"
> (8) "I hurt my knee," Jane said, "and it's bleeding!"

b. Quotation marks are used to emphasize a particular word or letter. Note: underlines may be used instead of quotation marks for letters.

> War knocks the "l" out of glory.
> She counted three "e's" in "cemetery."
> "Impossible" is an interesting word; most of it is possible.

c. Quotation marks are used around the titles of short literary works. Underline the titles of long literary works. (In print, underlines are italicized.)

> She read the poem, "The Raven," by Edgar Allan Poe.
> He read the novel, <u>David Copperfield</u>, by Charles Dickens.
> My favorite book is <u>Guns of Burgoyne</u> by Bruce Lancaster,
>   and my favorite chapter in this novel is "The River."

d. Quotation marks are used with dialogue. Notice that a new paragraph is formed every time the point of view shifts from one speaker to another.

> "Come to my party," Sue urged.
> Tom nodded. "I'd like to." He grinned. "Masquerade parties are fun! Besides, how can I say 'no' to you, Sue?"
> "Good!" Sue's lips puckered with an impish smile. "See you at seven, then."

e. Single quotation marks are used to indicate a quotation within a quotation.

> "My favorite poem," said Tim, "is 'If' by Rudyard Kipling."

f. Quotation marks may be used with a long quotation, one that is two paragraphs or more. Quotation marks are used at the BEGINNING of each paragraph, but at the end of the LAST paragraph only.

However—the preferred treatment of a long quotation is to indent the entire quotation, to switch from double spacing to single spacing, and to omit quotation marks.

Lincoln's Address at Gettysburg in 1863 is memorable. Schoolchildren memorize it, Fourth of July orators quote it, and newspaper editors refer to it.

> Fourscore and seven years ago our fathers brought forth on this continent a new nation, conceived in liberty and dedicated to the proposition that all men are created equal.
>
> Now we are engaged in a great civil war, testing whether that nation or any nation so conceived and so dedicated can long endure . . .

Whenever possible, follow the indented style for extended prose quotations and for more than two lines of poetry.

g. Periods and commas are always placed INSIDE end quotation marks.

(1) Bert promised, "We're going hunting tomorrow."
(2) "We're going hunting," Bert promised, "tomorrow."

Question marks and exclamation points are placed INSIDE or OUT-SIDE, depending on the sentence. (See 221-c, 229-b for additional examples.)

(3) Jay asked, "Can we go swimming tomorrow?" (The question mark goes with the question, inside the end quotation mark.)
(4) How do you spell "swimming"? (The question mark goes with the entire sentence, not with "swimming"; therefore the question mark goes outside the end quotation mark.)
(5) Jay asked, "How do you spell 'swimming'?" (The question mark is placed inside the double quotation mark, but outside the single quotation mark.)

226. APOSTROPHE

a. The **apostrophe** is used to indicate a missing letter or letters in a contraction.

can't (cannot)	don't (do not)
haven't (have not)	isn't (is not)
o'clock (of the clock)	won't (will not)

It is also used to indicate the omission of letters or numbers in other expressions.

> the Spirit of '76 (1776)
> the Class of '89 (1989)

b. The apostrophe is used to create the plural form of numbers, letters, and words being discussed.

> Jim wrote three "6's" on his paper.
> There are two "o's" in "kimono."
> Let there be no "if's," "and's," or "but's"!

c. The apostrophe is used to form the possessive case of nouns. (See 24.)

d. The apostrophe is used to turn time and money nouns into possessive adjectives.

> a week's work two weeks' work
> a dollar's worth two dollars' worth
> a day's work two days' work

227. DASH

The **dash** is stronger than the comma, indicating a longer pause or interruption.

a. The dash is used to signal an interruption.

> Carlos warned us that—oh, you aren't really interested!

b. Two dashes are used to separate a parenthetical expression from the rest of the sentence.

> Jane said—and I'm sure she's right—that our final exam is tomorrow.

c. Two dashes are used to separate appositives that contain commas.

> Three entries—chicken legs, spare ribs, and pork shoulder—are favorites at the annual Orthopedists' Banquet.

d. The dash is used for emphasis.

> With only one leg, Lonny walked—yes, walked—over a hundred miles.

> Rain makes flowers grow—and taxicabs disappear!

e. A short dash is used to indicate the omission of the word "to."

> She studied from 4–6 p.m. every day. (4 *to* 6)

> For tomorrow, read pages 18–105. (18 *to* 105)

f. A dash is used before a summarizing statement.

> He stopped for a small snack—a bowl of clam chowder, a pizza, an ice-cream sundae, and three eclairs.

228. PARENTHESES

a. Parentheses are used to enclose a parenthetical expression.

> Jane said (and I agree with her) that money doesn't talk these days—it goes without saying!

> More boys than girls are colorblind (see accompanying chart), but parents are not always aware of this.

b. Parentheses are used to indicate that a complete sentence is parenthetical: not a necessary part of the text.

> You can find all kinds of information about bubble gum in your school library. (Check the card catalog, the vertical file, and *Readers' Guide to Periodical Literature.*)

229. EXCLAMATION POINT

a. The **exclamation point** is used after words or sentences showing strong feeling. (Also see 76.)

> Help!
> Help me! I'm drowning!
> How beautiful you are!
> There are thirty muscles in a cat's ear!

b. The exclamation point is placed inside or outside quotation marks, depending on the sentence.

> Lopez shouted, "I'm drowning!" (The exclamation point goes with the quotation, and therefore is *inside* the quotation mark.)

> I hate the sound of the word "kiosk"! (The exclamation goes with the whole sentence, not with the word in quotation marks, and therefore is *outside* the quotation mark.)

230. HYPHEN

a. A **hyphen** is used to combine two words into a compound adjective when the adjective precedes a noun.

> a well-turned phrase
> an ill-qualified clerk

However—when the two words follow the noun, a hyphen is not used.

> a phrase well turned
> a clerk ill qualified

b. A hyphen is used in numbers from twenty-one to ninety-nine.

c. A hyphen is used after "half" when "half" is used as a prefix.

> half-aware   half-cocked   half-dollar

d. A hyphen is used to divide a word at the end of a line of writing. The word should always be divided at the end of a syllable.

> Both he and his friend decided to invest mon-
> ey in Treasury bonds.

> You should be especially careful not to mis-
> spell the word "misspell."

NEVER place a hyphen at the beginning of a new line.

231. UNDERLINING (In print, this appears as italics.)

a. Underline the titles of long literary works, such as novels and biographies, and of movies and TV shows.

> Margaret Mitchell's novel, *Gone With the Wind*, was origi-
> nally called *Tomorrow Is Another Day*.

> In 1939 Ernest Vincent Wright wrote a novel, *Gadsby*, which
> had not a single "e" in it.

b. Underline the titles of magazines and newspapers (but not articles before these titles unless the article is part of the title.)

> She reads *The New York Times* every day.

> He reads *Sports Illustrated* regularly.

c. Underline the names of works of art, of ships, and of planes.

> Her favorite painting is *Toledo* by El Greco.

> He named his yacht *Annabel* after his mother.

> One of the most famous planes in the world is the *Spirit of
> St. Louis*.

SPELLING

Most spelling rules have many exceptions, making them almost worthless. But a few have value. Here they are.

232. Prefixes

a. When adding a **prefix,** simply place it before the word. Retain the correct spelling of both word and prefix. For example: the word SPELL. Place the prefix before it—MIS. The correct spelling, then, is MISSPELL. Here are a few more examples.

> MIS + understood (MISunderstood)
>   + take (MIStake)
>
> IL + legal (ILlegal)
>   + legible (ILlegible)
>
> DIS + appoint (DISappoint)
>   + satisfy (DISsatisfy)
>
> IM + mediate (IMmediate)
>   + mature (IMmature)
>
> RE + commend (REcommend)
>   + hearse (REhearse)
>
> UN + usual (UNusual)
>   + necessary (UNnecessary)
>
> CO + operate (COoperate)
>   + ordinate (COordinate)
>
> PRE + paid (PREpaid)
>   + mature (PREmature)

b. Occasionally a hyphen is used after the prefix to prevent confusion. **Cooperate** is now accepted; so is **preempt.** But **copartner** may confuse, so it is usually written **co-partner.** When you are uncertain, check any good dictionary.

233. Suffixes

a. When adding a **suffix,** simply add it to the base word. Retain the correct spelling of both base word and suffix. For example: the word APPOINT. Add the suffix MENT for APPOINTMENT. Here are a few more examples.

> MENT + govern (governMENT)
>   + disappoint (disappointMENT)
>
> FUL + hope (hopeFUL)
>   + tear (tearFUL)
>
> ING + embarrass (embarrassING)
>   + cry (cryING)
>
> NESS + keen (keenNESS)
>   + cheerful (cheerfulNESS)
>
> LESS + care (careLESS)
>   + fear (fearLESS)
>
> *LY + final (finalLY)
>   + accidental (accidentalLY)
>   + critical (criticalLY)

Note well: Be sure to retain the ''-al'' when adding ''-ly'' to these adjectives.

b. If the suffix begins with a vowel and follows a silent ''e,'' drop the ''e.''

> hope + ing = HOPING
> guide + ance = GUIDANCE
> desire + able = DESIRABLE
> write + ing = WRITING

c. If the silent ''e'' follows a ''c'' or ''g,'' retain the ''e'' to keep the ''c'' or ''g'' soft.

> notice + able = NOTICEABLE
> change + able = CHANGEABLE
> courage + ous = COURAGEOUS
> peace + able = PEACEABLE

Exceptions: judgment; acknowledgment.

But: drop the "e" if the suffix begins with an "i" or "e."

> notice + ed = NOTICED
> notice + ing = NOTICING

d. If a word ends in a single consonant preceded by a single vowel, double the consonant when adding a suffix.

> occur + ed = OCCURRED
> plan + ing = PLANNING
> forget + ing = FORGETTING
> prefer + ed = PREFERRED

However—if the word is accented on the first syllable, do *not* double the consonant.

> profit + ed = PROFITED
> prefer + able = PREFERABLE
> benefit + ed = BENEFITED
> frighten + ing = FRIGHTENING

234. "EI"—"IE"

a. Start with the old rhyme:

> "i" before "e"
> except after "c"—
> or when sounded like "a"
> as in "neighbor" and "weigh."

b. The general rule is "i" before "e"—

> believe   fierce   thief   brief   wield

c. After "c," reverse the letters—

> receive   ceiling   deceive   conceit

d. When sounded like "a," reverse the letters—

> neighbor   weigh   freight   eight

Exceptions to (*b*): leisure, either, neither, height, veil, weird, seize, foreign.
Exception to (*c*): financier.

235. "Y" to "I"

a. If a word ends in "y" and the "y" is preceded by a consonant, change "y" to "i" when adding a suffix.

try—tried	study—studies
lonely—loneliness	beauty—beautiful
crazy—crazily	marry—marriage

Exceptions: dryness; shyness.

However—when adding "-ing," keep the "y."

try—trying	marry—marrying
dry—drying	study—studying

b. If the "y" is preceded by a vowel, keep the "y" when adding a suffix.

enjoy—enjoyed	employ—employment
prey—preying	display—displayed

Exceptions: day—daily; pay—paid; lay—laid.

236. WORDS ENDING IN "C"

If a word ends in "c," add a "k" before a suffix beginning with "e," "i," or "y."

picnic—picnicking—picnicked
mimic—mimicking—mimicked
panic—panicking—panicked—panicky

237

237. WORDS OFTEN MISSPELLED

absence	bicycle	cousin	encourage
accidentally	bookkeeping	criticism	engine
accommodate	business	criticize	enough
acquaintance		cruel	equipment
across	busy	curiosity	equipped
advertisement	calendar	curious	especially
again	campaign	current	essential
aisle	captain		executive
allotted	cemetery	customer	exercise
all right	century	daily	existence
	changeable	decision	
already	chaperon	defense	extraordinary
amateur	character	definitely	familiar
among	chocolate	descendant	famous
anonymous		description	fascinating
appearance	Christian	desirable	fashionable
Arctic	civilization	despair	fault
argument	climate	desperate	favorite
arithmetic	clothes		February
article	cocoa	develop	feminine
assassinate	college	dictionary	fierce
	colonel	difference	
athlete	colossal	diploma	figure
audience	column	disappear	finally
aunt	coming	disappoint	financially
author		discipline	flies
automobile	commitment	disease	foreign
autumn	committee	dissatisfied	fortunate
auxiliary	condemn	doesn't	forty
avenue	congratulate		fourth
awful	conscience	doubt	freight
awkward	conscientious	economical	friend
	consensus	ecstasy	
bachelor	constitution	eerie	fuel
banana	convenience	efficient	garage
banquet	cooperate	eighth	gazing
beauty		electricity	genealogy
beginning	cough	eligible	generous
believe	courageous	embarrass	genius
benefited	courteous	emphasize	genuine

Spelling 223

geography
glorious
gnawing

government
governor
graffiti
grammar
grate
grateful
gratitude
great
grief
grocery

guarantee
guess
gymnasium
handkerchief
handsome
happened
happiness
harassed
harbor
haven't

height
heroes
hesitate
history
hoarse
honor
hoping
horizon
horrible
hospital

humorous
husband
hymn
idea
ignorant

imagine
imitation
immediately
impossible
independent

Indian
individual
industrial
influence
initial
inoculate
insurance
interpretation
interrupt
interview

irrelevant
irresistible
island
jealous
jewelry
journey
judgment
justice
kimono
kitchen

knit
knock
knowledge
laboratory
language
laugh
lawyer
legislature
leisure
length

lesson
liaison
library

license
lieutenant
lightning
liquid
literature
living
loneliness

losing
lovable
luxurious
magazine
maneuver
marriage
masquerade
material
matinee
mayor

meant
medal
medicine
medieval
minimum
minuscule
minute
mischievous
missile
misspell

mortgage
movable
musician
naive
necessary
nickel
ninety
ninth
noticeable
nuisance

occasionally

occurred
often
omitted
parallel
particularly
pastime
peddler
penicillin
permanent

perseverance
personally
picnicking
planning
pneumonia
possession
possible
prejudice
privilege
probably

procedure
professor
pronunciation
psychology
questionnaire
realize
receive
recognize
recommend
referred

repetition
restaurant
rhythm
roommate
sacrilegious
sandwich
satisfactorily
schedule
scissors
secretary

seize
separate
sergeant
shining
similar
sincerely
sophomore
souvenir
specimen
success

sufficient
supersede

surprise
syllable
tariff
temperature
theater
thoroughly
tragedy
transferred

treasurer
truly
twelfth

tyranny
ukulele
undoubtedly
unforgettable
unmistakable
unnecessary
until

vacuum
vegetable
vengeance
vicinity

villain
weird
wheat
wholly
width
worst

writing
written
yesterday
yield
yolk

MNEMONIC AIDS

238. A **mnemonic aid** is any trick or clue that helps the memory. In spelling, mnemonic aids exist for many often-misspelled words.

For example: sepARATe is A RAT of a word. Once you have memorized this, you will never again misspell "separate."

Here is a short list of mnemonic aids. You may wish to create mnemonic aids for words that are a problem for you.

AGAIN   You will GAIN an A if you spell AGAIN correctly!

CEMETERY   Only "e's" are buried in a cEmEtEry.

CONSCIENCE   ConSCIENCE is not a matter of SCIENCE.

FEBRUARY   FeBRUary is a BRUtal month.

GRAMMAR   Don't MAR your gramMAR.

KIMONO   KIM and ONO wear KIMONOs.

LABORATORY   A LABORatory is a place where scientists LA-BOR.

LIBRARY   Spend time in a liBRAry and you will be a BRAin.

MEDIEVAL   It was easy to DIE in meDIEval times.

MINUSCULE   MINUS means less, so naturally there is a MINUS in MINUScule (which means "very small").

PIECE   Have a PIEce of PIE.

PRINCIPAL   A princiPAL is a PAL.

PRINCIPLE   A principLE of conduct is a ruLE.

SEPARATE   SepARATe is A RAT of a word.

VILLAIN   The VILLAin lives IN a VILLA.

NUMBERS

239. a. Write out whole numbers from one through ninety-nine. Write out any of the above followed by hundred, thousand, etc. Hyphens are required for numbers twenty-one through ninety-nine.

> eighty-seven cents
> three thousand dinosaurs
> seventy-one million yo-yos

Exceptions: very large numbers are usually written with a combination of number and word.

> 71.3 million
> $21 billion

b. Use numbers when more than two or three words would be required.

> $1.87 (not—one dollar eighty-seven cents)
> 3,256 dinosaurs
> 71,498,232 yo-yos

c. Use numbers if several numbers are clustered.

> Volumes I through V contain 231, 300, 242, 311, and 400 pages, respectively.

d. Ordinal numbers follow the above rules.

> She struck out in the bottom half of the ninth inning.
> He ranked sixteenth in his class.
> He ranked 165th in his class.

e. Do not begin a sentence with a number.

> Three children came to the party.
> Nineteen eighty-eight was a Presidential election year.

f. Numbers referring to the same type of item within a sentence or a paragraph should be uniform.

> Jill owns 23 books, Willy owns 217, and Sally owns 3. (The second number, 217, must be written as a number, so the other two follow suit. See 239-a, b.)

g. Use numbers for dates and street numbers. Notice the use of commas.

> Rae lived at 36 Broad Street from September 9, 1988, to October 1, 1989.

> Her address is 25 Pine Street, Merrydale, Ohio 00067.

Write out particular centuries and decades.

> nineteenth century (although 19th century is acceptable)
> during the seventies

Exception: if the century is specified for a decade, use numbers.

> during the 1970's

h. Form the plural of numbers by adding "'s." Quotation marks, although not required to form the plural, give emphasis to the number.

> There are three "2's" in this example.

BUT: During the seventies we prospered.

i. Capitalize the first half (but not the second half) of a hyphenated street name.

> Forty-second Street   Thirty-fourth Street

j. (1) Fractions standing alone or followed by "of a" or "of an" are spelled out and hyphenated.

> one-tenth   one-half inch
> three-fourths of an inch   one-hundredth

(2) However, numbers are used for fractions that are part of a modifier.

$\frac{1}{2}$-mile run $\frac{3}{4}$-inch pipe

(3) Numbers are used for fractions that would require more than two words.

$3\frac{1}{2}$ cartons $10\frac{1}{2}$ days

(4) If the fraction is the subject and is followed by "of," the verb agrees with the noun in the phrase.

One-fourth of the pizza *was* consumed.
One-fourth of the sandwiches *were* consumed.

k. If a noun indicates a measurement of space, time, or money, it is singular in meaning, even if it looks plural.

Ten dollars is the price he quoted.
Thirty minutes is all the time I can give you.
Five miles is the distance from Tantown to Tooley.

l. Mathematical expressions can be tricky when it comes to subject-verb agreement. Use the following as patterns.

Four TIMES two ARE eight.
Four AND two ARE six.
Four PLUS two IS six.
Four MINUS two IS two.
Four DIVIDED by two IS two.
ONE-FOURTH of four IS one.

REDUNDANCY

240. Redundancy refers to the use of more words than are necessary to express a meaning.

> **PAST history** (history is already past, so PAST is redundant and should be omitted)—just "history"
>
> **TRUE facts** (facts are true, so TRUE is redundant and should be omitted)—just "facts"
>
> **eliminate ALTOGETHER** (ALTOGETHER is redundant)
>
> **filled TO CAPACITY** (TO CAPACITY is redundant)
>
> **END result** (END is redundant)

In these other examples of redundancy, the capitalized words are unnecessary.

> attractive IN APPEARANCE
>
> square IN SHAPE
>
> blue IN COLOR
>
> never AT ANY TIME
>
> NEW innovation
>
> EARLY beginning (or FRESH beginning)
>
> repeat AGAIN
>
> biggest AND LARGEST
>
> MODERN car of tomorrow (or modern car OF TOMORROW)
>
> refers BACK to
>
> 3 p.m. IN THE AFTERNOON (or 3 a.m. IN THE MORNING)
>
> one SINGLE competitor
>
> may POSSIBLY be

Laugh Your Way Through Grammar

christened AS

fewer IN NUMBER

FREE gift

YOUNG infant

surgeon BY OCCUPATION

consensus OF OPINION

biography OF HIS LIFE

last OF ALL

continue ON

FINAL settlement

MUTUAL cooperation

SERIOUS danger

UNIVERSAL panacea

INDEX. The numbers following the entries refer NOT to page numbers but to item numbers in the text. By matching a reference number with a guide number (top, center, of each page in the text), you can locate any item quickly.

C

E

F

G

H

I

P

Participle (*continued*)
 past participle, formation of 41-a, b, d; 49-a
 present participle, formation of 49-a
Part of speech of a word depends on its use in a sentence 67
Parts of speech 1
 adjectives 52–56
 adverbs 57–63
 conjunctions 70–75
 interjections 76
 nouns 22–24
 prepositions 64–69
 pronouns 25–37
 verbs 38–51
Passed—past 176
Passive voice 45-b, c
Past participle (principal part of a verb) 41-a, b, d; 49-a
Past perfect tense 39-e
Past tense 39-b, 41
Peace—piece 177
Perfect tenses 39-d, e, f
Period 220
 after abbreviations and initials 220-b
 after declarative and imperative sentences 10-a, c; 220-a
 with quotation marks 220-c, 225-a, g
Person (first, second, third) of pronouns 26
 in conjugation of a verb 39
 in subject-verb agreement 47-a
Personal—personnel 178
Personal pronoun(s) 26, 27
Phenomenon—phenomena 23-o
Phrasal prepositions 66-b
Phrase(s) 5
 adjective 68-a
 adverb 68-b
 dangling verbal 51
 gerund 5, 50-b
 infinitive 5; 21-c; 48-c, d
 participial 5; 21-d; 49-d, e
 prepositional 5, 65
 restrictive and non-restrictive 224-l
 verb 4-e, 5
 verbal 51
Physics, singular number of 47-c
Piece—peace 177
Plenty: in subject-verb agreement 47-i
Plural
 nouns 23
 numbers, letters, words 23-n, 226-b
Plurality—majority 167

Politics, singular number of 47-c
Positive degree of comparison
 of adjectives 55-a
 of adverbs 62-a
Possessive adjective 35-d
Possessive case
 of nouns 24, 35-a
 of pronouns 35-b, d
Possessive case of nouns and pronouns used as adjectives 53-c
Pray—prey 179
Predicate 3, 4
 complete 3-d
 compound 11-a
 in a series (punctuation) 224-b
 simple 3-c, 11-a
 verb 3-b; 4-d, e, f
Predicate adjective 7-f; 44-a
Predicate noun 6-e.1; 7-f; 44-a; 48-d
Predicate pronoun 7-f; 33-d; 33-e.3, 4; 44-b
Predicate verb 3-b; 4-d, e, f
Prefix
 adding a prefix to a word 232-a, b
Preposition(s): a part of speech 64–69
 errors 69
 list of 66
 object of 64-b; see also ''Object of Preposition''
Prepositional phrase(s) 5, 65
 adjective and adverb 68
 affects subject-verb agreement 47-h, i, j, k
 in parallel structure 20-j
 in sentence combining 21-b
 punctuation of 224-e, h
Present participle, formation of 49-a
Present perfect tense 39-d
Present tense 39-a, 41
Prey—pray 179
Principal parts of verbs 41
 formation of 41-a
 misusing 41-d
 of irregular verbs (a list) 41-b, c
Principal—principle 180, 238
Pronoun(s): a part of speech 25–37
 agreement with antecedent 36
 case of 32–35
  nominative 33-a; also see ''Case: Nominative''
  objective 34-a; also see ''Case: Objective''
  possessive 35-b, c, d; also see ''Case: Possessive''
 errors 37

Laugh Your Way Through Grammar

SCORE SHEET (items 10–140)

10	91
11	92
12	93
13	94
14	95
15	96
16	97
20	98
21	99
23	100
24	101
27	102
29	103
30	104
31	105
33	106
34	107
35	108
36	109
37	110
39	111
40	112
41	113
45	114
46	115
47	116
48	117
49	118
50	119
55	120
56	121
62	122
63	123
69	124
74	125
75	126
77	127
78	128
79	129
80	130
81	131
82	132
83	133
84	134
85	135
86	136
87	137
88	138
89	139
90	140